"This book is a marvelous journey that tea̶ ̶.̶.̶.̶l̶k̶ ̶i̶n̶t̶o̶ the life of another while opening up new paths into our own life. The unlikely companionship of this African American woman writer and a white Catholic monk is one that few readers of this book will ever forget."

—**Dr. Willie James Jennings**, associate professor of theology
and Africana studies at Yale Divinity School; author of
After Whiteness: An Education in Belonging

"If you know Thomas Merton, you now must know Sophfronia Scott. In remarkable and marvelous ways, she invites us to complete our seeing of Merton—and also to see ourselves—by completing his humble seeing of a forgiving God."

—**Patricia Raybon**, author of *My First White Friend*
and *I Told The Mountain to Move*

"The beauty of this book is that . . . [Sophfronia Scott and Thomas Merton's] intimate conversations open outward to include anyone listening in, confident that what is deeply true about any of us is deeply true about all of us. Both Sophfronia Scott and Thomas Merton believe we belong to each other, and that faith frees us to speak frankly about our struggles with faith."

—**Barbara Brown Taylor**, *New York Times* bestselling author of
An Altar in the World, Learning to Walk in the Dark,
Holy Envy, and other books

"An exquisitely rendered account of the 'love affair' between an incandescent, twentieth-century flawed monk and a probing, twenty-first-century Black writer that brims with relevance and astonishing revelations. This book is a testament that if you seek, you indeed shall find."

—**Father Edward L. Beck, C.P.**, author and CNN commentator

"Sitting down with *The Seeker and the Monk* made me feel like I was overhearing a delightful conversation between two brilliant friends."
—**Carol Howard Merritt**, pastor of Bedford Presbyterian Church and author of *Healing Spiritual Wounds*

"A compelling, imaginative book to assist the world as we grapple with issues of race, racism, belonging, faith, hope, and love."
—**Rev. Nancy Lynne Westfield, PhD**, director, Wabash Center for Teaching and Learning in Theology and Religion

The Seeker and the Monk

The Seeker and the Monk

EVERYDAY CONVERSATIONS with THOMAS MERTON

SOPHFRONIA SCOTT

Foreword by Barbara Brown Taylor

BROADLEAF BOOKS

MINNEAPOLIS

THE SEEKER AND THE MONK
Everyday Conversations with Thomas Merton

Cover art: Brad Norr
Cover design: Brad Norr

Print ISBN: 978-1-5064-6496-1
eBook ISBN: 978-1-5064-6497-8

In loving memory of
Katherine Kjellgren
Your voice forever with me

Contents

Foreword

ANYONE WHO HAS PRACTICED FAITH KNOWS THERE IS both an inside and an outside to it. To come inside after a long time outside is to find community, solace, and shelter. Depending on what kind of faith it is, a comforting blanket of certainty may be in the welcome bag—along with a clear set of expectations about how insiders behave.

After a while, however, some of us find the community too chatty or the enclosure too small. Inside doesn't look the same from the inside as it did from the outside. Perhaps we just want to stretch our legs and be alone outside for a while, for reasons as mysterious as the ones that led us to come inside in the first place.

Thomas Merton knew all about that. So does Sophfronia Scott, who met Merton in his journals more than forty years after his death. Like him, she is gripped by the sacred. Like him, she writes divinely about being human. Like him, she knows the push and pull of faith, the view from both sides of the enclosure. Small wonder, then, that her sense of connection to Merton was instant. Hearing his work read out loud for the first time, she felt something open up inside her. "It felt immense and small at the same time," she writes in the pages that follow, "because it felt like one word: *Yes*. Yes, I thought. That's exactly it."

You are likely to think the same thing as you listen to the conversations she strikes up with him in this book, as full of give-and-take as if he were right beside her. There is none of the usual deference to a famous teacher. There is nothing timid in the dialogues she has with Merton about possessions, prayer, ambition, and social justice. When she talks with him about racism, it is as if they are sitting on his porch with yesterday's newspaper spread between them. When she speaks with him about death, it is with the gravity of someone who knows she is the same age now as Merton was when he died.

It is easy to forget that these are conversations between a monk and a seeker. When Sophfronia calls him "Thomas" and offers him "loving correction," it begins to sound more like a holy heart-to-heart that spans gender, race, vocation, history, and religious tradition. Spanning these differences may sound less grand to you than transcending them, but the distinctions between this particular monk and this particular seeker are too precious to be eclipsed. They prove that like-spirited people need not be alike. They show how people coming at faith from separate directions can still reach for each other's hands when they make a run for it. Whether they are on their ways in or out of their comfort zones, they recognize each other as kin.

The beauty of this book is that I now feel the same way about them. Their intimate conversations open outward to include anyone listening in, confident that what is deeply true about any of us is deeply true about all of us. Both Sophfronia Scott and Thomas Merton believe we belong to each other, and that faith frees us to speak frankly about our struggles with faith.

Wherever you are on your sacred way—rejoicing in new-found community or walking alone in the woods—you have found two new conversation partners who know all about it. Between them and the Spirit that unites them, they have you covered.

—Barbara Brown Taylor, *New York Times* bestselling author of *An Altar in the World, Learning to Walk in the Dark, Holy Envy*, and other books

1

This Monk Who Follows Me Around

GETTING TO KNOW THOMAS MERTON

Of one thing I am certain. My life must have meaning. This meaning springs from a creative and intelligent harmony between my will and the will of God—a clarification by right action. But what is right action? What is the will of God? What are the sources of all my confusion on these?

A FEW YEARS AGO, A FRIEND OF MINE SHARED IN MY SOCIAL media feed a Thomas Merton quote he'd come across in his reading. He added this comment to me: *There's your boy.*

I stared at the words for several minutes. Was Thomas Merton my "boy"? How could that be possible? Obviously my friend was having a good time needling me. As he could see from my Goodreads updates, I read a lot of Merton. Every so often I'd quote him too. But the "my boy" thing knocked me upside the head with its incongruity.

Thomas Merton was a white Catholic monk who lived most of his life in a monastery in Kentucky and died over fifty years ago. I'm a Black woman, not Catholic but Episcopalian, with Baptist notes from my childhood. We have nothing in common other than Ivy League educations (mine from Harvard, his from Columbia) and a searching nature when it comes to faith. I am a seeker into the mystery of what tethers my life to the divine, and I long to see the notes of grace scattered in the crevices of experience, to learn how to read those messages, continually saying, "I love you anyway." I want to talk of these things with a like-minded being. And yet if I met him today at a cocktail party, I'd probably find Merton boisterous and slightly boorish. Later I'd likely describe him to friends as having that entitled, mansplaining kind of tone that makes you keep your distance.

But then another friend asked me to join her on a panel about Thomas Merton for the Festival of Faith and Writing at Calvin College in Grand Rapids, Michigan. When I sat down onstage, it hit home that my fellow panelists were theologians or academic scholars. Merton's work is taught and studied worldwide. He left behind a voluminous collection of writing: dozens of books, essays, articles, lectures, and so much written correspondence it would choke an email inbox. He's considered a model of the pursuit of Christian faith and an influential voice on matters of social justice, race, religion, and activism. And his prophetic thoughts in these areas still ring true today. Pope Francis, in a speech to the US Congress, called Merton "a thinker who challenged the certitudes of his time and opened new horizons for souls and for the Church. He was also a man of dialogue, a promoter of peace between peoples and religions."

So I felt impelled to tell the audience right away that I was not a scholar. "I just have this monk who follows me around," I said. "And he kind of mentors me and gives me advice." I described the strong sense I have of an ongoing dialogue with Merton as I forge along on my spiritual journey. I've had with him moments of learning, affirmation, surprise, and even disagreement. The more I spoke about him, the more I felt myself settling into the realization that, yes, I suppose he is "my boy"—and someone who has, across the many years and many differences between us, managed to become a dear friend.

TORN PAGES

I first met Thomas Merton in December 2011. I was at the start of a graduate program in which I would earn my master of fine arts in creative writing when I heard a lecturer, Robert Vivian, quote an extended passage from Merton's *Conjectures of a Guilty Bystander*. The section called "The Night Spirit and the Dawn Air" begins with "How the valley awakes..." Hearing those words, to put it simply, set my world on fire:

> The first chirps of the waking birds mark the *"point vierge"* of the dawn under a sky as yet without real light, a moment of awe and inexpressible innocence, when the Father in perfect silence opens their eyes. They begin to speak to Him, not with fluent song, but with an awakening question that is their dawn state, their state at the *"point vierge."* Their condition asks if it is time for them to "be." He answers "yes." Then,

they one by one wake up, and become birds. They manifest themselves as birds beginning to sing. Presently they will be fully themselves, and will even fly.

Meanwhile, the most wonderful moment of the day is that when creation in its innocence asks permission to "be" once again, as it did on the first morning that ever was.

Suddenly I wanted to be outside at the crack of dawn, eager to sense the voice of the Creator Spirit giving the waking birds this vital message, their cue: it is time for you to be. I too wanted God to tell me it was time for *me* to be. Merton goes on to say, "Here is an unspeakable secret: paradise is all around us and we do not understand." I felt something open up in my whole being. It felt immense and small at the same time because it felt like one word: *Yes. Yes*, I thought. *That's exactly it.*

I was so fascinated by what I'd heard that I immediately searched for the book in the online catalog at my local library. Notice that I didn't buy the book, which I could have easily done in the moment. I was intrigued by Merton, but not enough to invest in him. As it turned out, the library didn't have *Conjectures*, but I could borrow the book via interlibrary loan. I requested it and waited—and waited some more. When I received the email saying the book had finally arrived, I drove straight to the library, retrieved the book from the "holds" shelf, and opened it right there and then. That's how eager I was to see in print the words I'd heard, to see if they were as beautiful on the page as they had felt in my ears.

I couldn't find them.

I flipped through the book again, and again, but I couldn't find the passage. I thought perhaps I'd gotten the name of the book wrong, or maybe the lecturer had mistakenly quoted a different Merton book. But then I noticed some ragged edges of paper, deep in the spine, and I realized: the very pages I sought *had been torn out*!

Call me crazy, but I took this as a sign. I felt as though something were telling me this wouldn't be casual curiosity. If the pages had been there, I may have read them but not finished the whole book. I may have read the part I was seeking and then tossed the book aside—kind of like picking an apple in an orchard and only taking one bite. The fact that those very pages I was seeking were precious enough to another reader that they had kept them—well, it seemed like I was at the beginning of something, something that required more of my time and attention.

So I purchased *Conjectures* and then the autobiography that made Merton famous, *The Seven Storey Mountain.* I dove into *Mountain* first. I wanted to know who this Merton guy was and how he came to write his soul-searing words. He wrote *Mountain* when he was only thirty-one years old and fewer than five years into the monastic life. I learned he was born in France in 1915. His parents were artists. His mother, a Quaker, died when he was six. His father, from New Zealand, had Merton baptized in the Church of England. Merton's only sibling, a brother, was killed in action during World War II. As a teen, Merton had no real home, going from boarding school to attend Cambridge, where he was intent on studying drinking and women more than anything else. When he fathered a child out of wedlock (he never met the child, who, according to longtime Merton friend Jim Knight, was killed during a World War II German air raid on London), Merton's frustrated guardian finally had enough and sent him to live with relatives in America—Long Island, Queens. Merton entered Columbia University and seemed ready to continue his trail of indiscretions. But this time his studies included spirituality and religion. Eventually, he writes, he became "overwhelmed with a sudden and profound insight into the misery and corruption of [his] own soul" and converted to Roman Catholicism. He was twenty-three years old.

Despite his poor behavior, there was something about Merton the person I liked right away. He reminded me of some of my Harvard classmates—a quick mind with multiple talents and interests. He could draw, he could write, he loved reading, he played sports, and he loved jazz. Once he converted, I was impressed with his ongoing praise of the saints and his complete embrace of the Holy Virgin Mary. I couldn't fathom how he had been a nonbeliever. Because he didn't just convert. It's like he willingly jumped off a cliff, fully in love, placing his heart into something he could barely understand and trusting that something—or someone—would uphold him. That is my sense of faith too, and this sense drew me ever closer to him. I wanted to talk to him about it. And I knew he wouldn't be silent because I could tell he was a talker, ready to engage with any topic.

In fact, maybe it was the sense that he was such a talker that made me feel like something was missing in *The Seven Storey Mountain*. There were places where he seemed to be equivocating, or speaking in generalities instead of in detail about certain events. The out-of-wedlock child, for example, I learned of elsewhere. He only writes about the results of the indiscretion.

In one instance, it seemed this kept him from being accepted into the first monastic order he tried to enter, the Franciscans. He referred only to "who [he] had been" and said, "I seemed to have forgotten that I had ever sinned," and then he discussed how he had been asked to withdraw his application to the Franciscans. For what? I wondered. For being a college-age drinker? It didn't make sense. I felt as though I were getting only a muted version of the author.

At first, I thought it was just me and my creative writing teacher antennae in overdrive. But a few months later, while browsing in my church's library, I came across Michael Mott's 1984 biography, *The Seven Mountains of Thomas Merton*. In perusing the 770-page tome, I learned my intuition had been right. Merton's book (all of his published work, actually) had to go through approved channels of the Catholic Church—essentially, through a censorship process. This process wasn't unique to Merton, but he certainly gave the censors enough to keep them quite busy. In 1952, his book *The Sign of Jonas* was initially banned from publication. In 1962, as his attention turned toward nuclear war and peace, he was told to stop writing on the topic—it was unbecoming of a monk.

I also learned from Mott of a treasure trove: Merton had left behind extensive journals, seven volumes in all, with the stipulation in his will that they not be published until twenty-five years after his death. I hit the internet as soon as I could and tracked down the seven journals for myself. I had sensed a humanity about him that *The Seven Storey Mountain* only hinted at. No, more than that—I felt if I could find Merton's true voice, I might find a kindred spirit, perhaps even a friend.

In his journals, that is exactly what I found.

THE PRIVATE MERTON

Merton's journals—which begin in 1939, when he was in his early twenties, before he entered the monastery, and detail his life's journey, with only a few pauses, up until a few days before his death in Thailand—pierced through the labels of monk, mystic, and prophet and brought him to my side. He became "Thomas" to me, a flesh-and-blood companion. I call him Thomas and will continue to, at times, address him directly as such in these pages, because it feels right to me. It's also how he responded during a 1940 encounter with two little girls in Havana, Cuba, who asked him his name. "Thomas. What's yours?" he responded.

This was a man who did not see himself as special, who struggled to find and understand his place in God's creation, who wanted to be worthy of Christ's sacrifice, who expressed the very human emotions of doubt, anger, disappointment, and boredom. At another point in the journals, he wrote about a regular meeting, called *chapter*, of his entire monastic community. "This morning had to talk in chapter about the Psalms of Sext," he wrote. "I am not so bored in chapter when I am the one talking."

Yes, he made me laugh. He had his petty complaints: He didn't like the sound of the choir, and advertising bugged him. He read ads in a "What is this world coming to?" kind of way. He didn't like it when people came to a jazz club and talked through the music instead of listening. It was fascinating to observe him in his formative twenties. He balanced a busyness and playfulness, always seeking to read even as he was writing and teaching in addition to hanging out with his friends. His brash reviews of the art he saw at the World's Fair in Queens and of the books he'd read showed a brilliant mind at work, often with a youthful impatience: "I suppose if Melville Cain was to repeat the question to me this minute I'd give back the same answer. On the other hand I believe if W. H. Auden was to walk in the room and dare me to like the works of Melville Cain I would stand up and like them just fine. . . . No I wouldn't, I was just fooling."

The youthful Merton could also be tedious and melodramatic, especially right before he entered the Abbey of Gethsemani, the monastery in Kentucky where he lived much of his life. However, he knew enough to be sorry: "There are a lot of things I wish I had never said, because they were foolish, or because they hurt people, or because they were intended to. But mostly because they were absurd."

Reading the journals gave me the mostly unvarnished Merton I sought. I say *mostly* because he sometimes edited himself, tearing out pages after he wrote them. I won't blame Merton for this—in fact, it endeared him to me more because he proved to be no different from other brash, confused young men. I loved his account of his travel to Cuba, of the saints with whom he became enamored, and of his struggle to figure out how exactly he was meant to serve God. He admitted, "I have a natural tendency to become an escapist, a snob, a narcissist. (And my problems arise largely from guilt and attempts to cover up this guilt from myself and others.)" Three years later, on the fourteenth anniversary of his ordination to the priesthood, he took inventory and counted himself as falling short:

I have certainly not been a model of priestly virtue. It does not seem that I have willfully sinned, i.e. with my eyes wide open, in a serious matter. But there have been repeated failures, failures without number, like holes appearing everywhere in a worn-out garment. Nothing has been effectively patched. The moths have eaten me, while I was confusedly intent on what seemed to be good, or important—or necessary for survival. . . .

Lately I have been uncharitable and unjust. . . .

I have not always been temperate, and if I go to town and someone pours me a drink, I don't resist another or even a third. And I have sometimes gone beyond the *trivium perfectum* [the perfect third]. A monk?

√ Probably the chief weakness has been lack of real courage to bear up under the attrition of monastic and priestly life. Anyway, I am worn down. I am easily discouraged. The depressions are deeper, more frequent. I am near fifty. People think I am happy.

Thomas, I thought when I read this passage, *please allow me to be Lucy to your Charlie Brown. The fact that you realize you have a problem means you're not too far gone. (Five cents, please!)* Indeed, when he could have ripped out or simply not written about the most shocking aspect of his monk's life—the love he shared with a young woman he refers to as "M.," a nurse he met when recovering from back surgery during the spring of 1966—he notes, specifically, that he will not omit their story. "I have no intention of keeping the M. business entirely out of sight. I have always wanted to be completely open, both about my mistakes and about my effort to make sense out of my life," he writes. "The affair with M. is an important part of it—and shows my limitations as well as a side of me that is—well, it needs to be known too, for it is part of me. My need for love, my loneliness, my inner division, the struggle in which solitude is at once a problem and a 'solution.' And perhaps not a perfect solution either." He wanted all of himself to be known, including his messy and sometimes embarrassing adventure of learning to love, perhaps for the first time in his life. I was fascinated by the vulnerability he was willing to show.

This was the person I wanted to learn from, and this is the material I dialogue with most in this book. I have also sought out his letters, and yes, I consult his traditionally known works—the early works that continue to provide spiritual food for those hungering for a path to connection. These include *The Sign of Jonas* and *New Seeds of Contemplation*, as well as his later works of activism: *Seeds of Destruction, Raids on the Unspeakable*, and *Conjectures of a Guilty Bystander*.

But it is the unvarnished Merton of the seven private journals—my Thomas—I converse with. He understands my bewilderment with politics, my desire to place ambition in its proper sphere. He knows my frustrations with holding out hope for my country's racial consciousness despite the delusions that abound. I want to share ideas with him about the mysterious activity called prayer and how one goes about reviving faith exhausted by trying times. I feel he has something to say about how we care for our earthly environment and why it's important to our souls. I want to talk about the possibility of transcendence, the very taste and feel of it, and its reverberating certainty of God all around us.

"The ever-changing reality in the midst of which we live should awaken us to the possibility of an uninterrupted dialogue with God," he writes in *New Seeds of Contemplation*. "By this I do not mean continuous 'talk,' . . . but a dialogue of love and of choice. A dialogue of deep wills." I like to think Thomas and I have such a dialogue. Don't get me wrong—I'm not equating him with the divine. In fact, at times he seems like a man out to "hack" life, wanting to outsmart everything and everyone, even death. I take him to task in such moments. When he describes a Zen teaching on the power of sincerity or non-deceiving, he observes, "This power of non-deceiving is, for me, the all important thing and I lack it. That is, I have the seeds of it but I do not let them grow. I begin to want to *assure* people of my sincerity, and then I deceive myself. And, of course, I am trying to deceive them—that I am sincere."

Thomas, I think to myself (and to him), *I think this shows a lack of love for others. You think yourself smarter than everyone else so even when you mean well, you think you will be misunderstood. So you have to double explain, hide, deceive. You don't trust them, nor do you really trust what is in your own heart. That sounds like a tiring way to be.*

THE WHY OF MERTON

But despite these issues, knowing Thomas helps me access and love the impossible world—to listen to the hope in birdsong, to go about my business with the playful diligence of a squirrel. To clear the trees in my life and not a forest when I need vision. To weed a patch of earth and find God. To understand that any consumer purchase requires something of my head and heart, not just my wallet, and needs spiritual consideration. To trust that I can and should have a voice in what I see going on in the world and that my voice—and everyone else's—matters. To constantly seek the revelation that he himself experienced of loving and being one with the world. To stare into the face of racism and not allow it to touch my capability to love and believe in the unity inherent in our humanity, that we are indeed all one. To think of death not as something to fear but as a journey for which I must continually prepare with ordered thinking and loving prayer.

I know I'm not the first to feel this way—to sense that in the life and writings of this twentieth-century monk, there is wisdom to be gleaned for those of us living in the twenty-first. The author Sue Monk Kidd, who feels her own connection to Merton, writes, "His life became a remarkably clear lens through which others glimpse their own self, especially the self their soul most demands. So, even before we reached the hermitage, it occurred to me I may have sculpted a personal image of Merton that had as much to do with my *own* longing to be, as it did with his."

I too have constructed my own image of Merton in these pages. I see him in a certain way, filtered through a lens colored by who I am and what I have experienced. But isn't that always the way it is? We all can have such different impressions of each other. I offer my Merton image so he may be available to someone else, who will then craft their own.

I've always felt my job is to offer a way of looking at things. To model a way of living just by being. I'm not in a position to tell people what to do, and I wouldn't want to be. But I can share what I know, what I've figured out. *Take that path and be careful of the brambles on the right, the poison ivy near your feet. There's a fantastic view of the valley, but you have to step through heavy brush to see it.*

I've been asked, "Are you ordained?" but the answer is always no. That's not my job. I believe it is my specific vocation not to be ordained, to model how a layperson can engage with faith, the Bible, and Christ. I'm like a scout on the spiritual frontier. I send back missives in my writing.

Thomas shows me there is a weird dance to be done, a kind of engagement with the world while having to stand apart from it. And I perform it with him in a variety of roles. So I take him as I would my son in the frivolity of his youth, offering loving correction when I think he should know better; and as I would one of my brothers in all their brashness; and as a kindred spirit known as *anam cara* in all the wisdom, bitterness, and then wonder of middle age. I recognize his changes until it feels as though we have grown up together.

In fact, we—he and I—are the same age now. Merton was only fifty-three when he died in Bangkok, Thailand, while attending a monastic conference. His cause of death is listed as accidental electrocution, the result of him touching a faulty fan after getting out of a shower. And I feel a tremendous sadness that he's gone. I'm longing for an old friend.

But the words he left behind make Merton present and, as this book will show, a necessary voice for our times. For all seekers, he offers us a way into appreciating our own humanity and discovering that our flaws could be the very things that connect us most to what is perfect and divine. He is not distant, not separated from us by multiple centuries and another time. He is recent, and he looked through a window in which he saw our times. He is someone to whom you can bring the questions of your life, large and small, and he has something to say because he has experienced it himself or thought about it deeply.

I invite you into the questioning journey of these pages. May his wisdom enrich your own journey, but really, as Merton has said, we are all one spirit. We are in union. We are all walking this path together.

2

Alexa, Where's My Stuff?
WHEN WHAT WE OWN OWNS US

Our material riches unfortunately imply a spiritual, cultural, and moral poverty that are perhaps far greater than we see.

IN DECEMBER 1941, WHEN A YOUNG THOMAS MERTON was preparing to travel to Kentucky in hopes that the monks there would accept him into the Abbey of Gethsemani, he disposed of his things. He boxed up most of his clothing and donated it to a charity in Harlem. He gave away most of his books. He closed his checking account and collected his remaining pay from his teaching job at St. Bonaventure's, a college located in Olean, New York. He writes, "All my possessions fitted into one suitcase, and that was too much."

Once he was clothed in the postulant's habit, after turning over his fountain pen, wristwatch, and pocket cash, he doesn't mention the contents of this suitcase again. In fact, he writes, "And so within three days of my admission to the novitiate I was out of my secular clothing and glad to get rid of it for ever [*sic*]."

I was impressed by how willing he was to let go of his things. Surely he took to heart Luke 12:15, where Jesus says that "life does not consist in the abundance of possessions." And yet I can tell you what I took with me to college, because it did feel as though I were packing up my life. I had a suitcase of clothing, much of it bought for school with funds I'd earned that summer as an aide in my town's Social Security office. I also brought with me a three-speed bicycle my father had bought for me on a payment plan from a bike shop and five boxes—none particularly large—containing books, posters, and various keepsakes I'd collected during my childhood and high school years. Actually, the boxes didn't need packing—this was how I'd stored my belongings at home. When you grow up with six siblings in a house that's less than a thousand square feet, you learn how to protect your things.

These items contained something of my identity and carried enough meaning that if I had had to part with them upon my arrival at Harvard, as Thomas had to do upon his arrival at the monastery, I'm not sure I would have known how to do it. In fact, three years later when my bike was stolen, I cried for days over the loss of something that, for me, had symbolized my father's love. My attachment was innocent, coming from a place of having little. But I do see the problem of gaining more possessions as one grows into adulthood and still imbuing these items with the importance of our identity and our connection to the world.

Merton recognized this problem and commented on it throughout his life without his stance ever changing. He appreciated the magnitude of an issue that he discerned would cause harm in two major ways: by disrupting our connection to God and by being the foundation for violence—the general disruption of peace—in our world. He saw the danger not in having too much stuff (although that's an issue as well) but in how much we are spiritually invested in our possessions. ✔ This is what Jesus meant when he said, after observing the disappointment of a rich man whom he exhorted to dispose of his possessions and follow him, "It is easier for a camel to go through the eye of a needle than for someone who is rich to enter the kingdom of God" (Matt 19:24). The man valued his connection to his belongings above closeness to Christ and, through him, God.

Merton writes, "Our trouble is that we are alienated from our own personal reality, or true self. We do not believe in anything but money and the power or the enjoyment which come from the possession of money. We do not believe in ourselves, except in so far as we can estimate our own worth, and verify, by our operations in the world of the market, that our subjective price coincides with what society is willing to pay for us."

IDOL WORSHIP

As a society, we've come to a place where what we own owns us. Our possessions dictate our thoughts and actions. We purchase or long for bigger homes with more storage space rather than considering whether we should have fewer belongings. We can't get rid of things because of the value, real or otherwise, that we perceive in them. And yet we still have the desire to buy more things—bigger, better, newer, flashier things. According to writer Joshua Becker in his book *The Minimalist Home*, Americans spend $1.2 trillion annually on nonessential goods. The worst part is that this desire is so common that we're not aware of it or of its controlling interest in our lives, something Merton also observed in his time: "The great sin, the source of all other sin, is idolatry and never has it been greater, more prevalent, than now. Yet it is almost completely unrecognized precisely because it is so overwhelming and so total. It takes in everything. There is nothing else left. Fetishism of power, machines, possessions, medicines, sports, clothes, etc., all kept going by greed for money and power."

Have we made idols of our possessions?

What is an idol? It's an object of worship—something loved and revered, which means you look upon the thing with a certain amount of emotion. Think of the golden calf in Exodus, the idol worshipped by the Jewish people when they thought their leader, Moses, was dead. The idol captivates the eye. I don't feel there is sin in making a purchase, because I believe sin is what separates us from God, and one purchase wouldn't necessarily do that. But too much of something can separate us from God—like making multiple purchases and then continually thinking about when you can go shopping again to make another purchase, whether or not you need or can afford it. That's why gluttony is one of the seven deadly sins. Overindulgence—steeping one's self in one thing, like food or clothing or alcohol or drugs—can separate you from God. This is how addiction works. It's a sole focus on having that one thing again and again to the detriment of all else in one's life. The one thing becomes like an idol. When that idol replaces God, that's where the real trouble lies.

One bit of comfort is that we aren't totally at fault in this. We don't realize our desire is ongoing because we are reacting to stimuli that continually bombard us with messages and images of all the beautiful things we can buy and the beautiful lives we can have as a result. Merton saw this manipulation, much to his ire. He recognized the problem of advertising, of having images and the promise of products constantly dangled before us. In Louisville in December 1958, before Christmas, he noted, "The overwhelming welter of meaningless objects, goods, activities—The indiscriminate chaotic nest of 'things' good, bad and indifferent, that pour over you at every moment—books, magazines, food, drink, women, cigarettes, clothes, toys, cars, drugs. Add to this the anonymous, characterless, 'decoration' of the town for Christmas and the people running around buying things for no reason except that now is a time [in] which everybody buys things."

THE COVETING EYE

Merton saw that we are at the mercy of products incessantly paraded in front of us in ads and shop windows, in commercials and in the mail. He knew that what we see is where our heads and hearts will go. This is what it means to covet. In the film *The Silence of the Lambs*, serial killer Hannibal Lecter (Anthony Hopkins) asks of FBI agent Clarice Starling (Jodie Foster), "How do we begin to covet, Clarice?" He provides the answer: "We begin by coveting what we see every day."

When I lived in New York City, I lived, without realizing it, in an ongoing state of coveting. These days, living in

Connecticut, I don't shop much. I used to think it was because I don't hang out at malls, and since I work from home, I rarely buy clothes unless I'm replacing something I've worn out, like jeans. But then one day when I was back in Manhattan for a meeting, I had some time on my hands, so I walked to my meeting instead of taking the subway. It was one of those gorgeous, eye-popping days in which everything you look at seems bright and shiny and promising—and in Manhattan, that includes shop windows. In Manhattan, you stroll past stores the same way you would in a mall. Only it doesn't stop. You see store after store offering everything your heart could desire, from clothing to bedding and from books to artwork. Think bikes and mirrors, running shoes and blenders. Suddenly I noticed myself noticing what was in the windows—the colors, the trends, the accessories. I felt delight from a slick pair of boots, from the texture and pattern of an interesting coat, from the cut of a beautiful dress. I imagined what it would be like to buy these things—and I realized how, once upon a time, I did.

I thought about the clothing I'd bought in the past, how it was often a result of walking past these windows regularly. Even if I didn't purchase an item right away, seeing it every day only heightened my desire. I think it's because I have a vibrant imagination. If I see something I like, I can imagine myself wearing it. I see myself walking through the airport, walking down the street, standing at the microphone. In the movie of my life, the stylist and set dresser of my mind are quickly activated and always hard at work. *That coat would be perfect for the conference this spring.* I was probably in a constant state of desire, and definitely I had been coveting.

22

Is this the heart of materialism? I'm thinking about what we all have and why we have it, because now we can "see" more items than ever before. If Merton thought "the chaotic nest of things" was pouring over us then, today we have a deluge—perhaps even a tidal wave. We can buy anything at any hour of the day. Where once we had to go to a physical location to shop or wait for catalogs to come in the mail to order an item, now we can browse stores on television and on our computers without leaving home. We can buy the same way, punching in our credit card numbers from the comfort of our plush living room sectionals. A quick call out to a smart speaker device—"Alexa, where's my stuff?"—will tell you when the goods are on the way. I'm guessing the time it takes from the start of coveting to the actual purchase is a lot shorter now, especially since, once Google or social media sniffs your interest, your screen and newsfeed will be filled with ads for the handbag or shoes you'd only been curious about before.

THE CONSEQUENCES

Remember, it's not just buying all the stuff. It's our attachment to our stuff that enslaves us. Think of the character of Carl in the animated film *Up*, who spends most of the plot tethered to his home and belongings and suspended in the air by a multitude of helium balloons. He eventually learns he can't help others or move forward with his life until he's willing to let go of his possessions. It's a fitting illumination of Christ's words: "Where your treasure is, there your heart will be also" (Matt 6:21).

Carl's hold on what he cared about meant his hands were too full to accept or understand divine spirit.

And this is the danger Christ seeks to protect us from. He exhorts us to give not only as a way of being charitable but as a way of letting go—of freeing ourselves from the idolatry of our possessions. "If anyone wants to sue you and take your coat, give your cloak as well," Jesus tells his listeners. "Give to everyone who begs from you, and do not refuse anyone who wants to borrow from you" (Matt 5:40, 42). In doing so, you give away the thing and your attachment to it, the very aspect that would separate you from God.

It would be easy to take this lightly. After all, what harm is there in a car, a bracelet, a collection of basketball shoes, an exquisite painting, or a nice washer and dryer? Individually, perhaps none. But collectively, what we own takes up so much of our consciousness that we can be pushed to extremes to protect it all. During a time when the world seemed to be on the brink of nuclear war, Merton read about a man in Chicago: "[He] has (like a million others) built himself a fallout shelter in his cellar, and has declared that he and his family will occupy it keeping everyone else out, if necessary, with a machine gun. This I think is the final exaltation of the American way of life: individualism, comfort, security, and to hell with everybody else." Today we see this same behavior—think of the images every Thanksgiving of Black Friday shoppers stampeding over each other to get through store doors so they can fight over discounted merchandise. Or the scenes during the COVID-19 pandemic of people arguing over toilet paper and paper towels and, even worse, brandishing rifles during protests against the halting of commerce. In their determination to protect what's theirs, they forget their connectedness to the well-being of others.

And such violence can resonate beyond ourselves, into the world at large. Thomas so carefully laid out the path, showing how the stories and thoughts we have about a powerful possession can lead to greater suffering. His example—the car—is well suited. It is the one possession that can signal our age, marital status, economic situation, and even mental state—how many midlife crises have been launched with the purchase of a red convertible? He writes, "The attachment of the modern American to his automobile, and the *symbolic* role played by his car, with its aggressive and lubric design, its useless power, its otiose gadgetry, its consumption of fuel, which is advertised as having almost supernatural power . . . this is where the study of American mythology should begin."

In fact, he claims a space for the car in the annals of societal decline: "Meditation on the automobile, what it is used for, what it stands for—the automobile as weapon, as self-advertisement, as brothel, as a means of suicide, etc.—might lead us at once right into the heart of all contemporary American problems: race, war, the crisis of marriage, the flight from reality into myth and fanaticism, the growing brutality and irrationality of American mores."

Notice what happens when we collectively release our active use of and attachment to our vehicles, something we all witnessed during the COVID-19 pandemic. We spent less money on gas, and oil prices plummeted. We stopped polluting the air. In fact, all over the country, views once dimmed by smog became serenely clear. Pike's Peak could be seen from northwest Denver, Colorado, a distance of over one hundred miles. What else might we see more clearly if we could hold our stuff more loosely?

ONE JACKET, ONE NEW CONSCIOUSNESS

How do we bring ourselves to do that? We can pray. Merton's own written prayers included this one: "Stanch in me the rank wound of covetousness and the hungers that exhaust my nature with their bleeding." But we have to understand what the prayer is truly for. It's not about beating yourself up for wanting nice things. It's not about not buying that new car if your family needs it. This is about a remaking of our consciousness—to move from one way of thinking and being to an entirely different way. And I believe it could start with a jacket—one denim jacket.

When I visited the Thomas Merton Center at Bellarmine University in Louisville, Kentucky, I stood for a while in front of the display holding Thomas's denim jacket, the one he wore in so many photos. It's plain. The cuffs are frayed and the color faded, particularly at the elbows. It has four pockets: two large ones at the bottom and two smaller ones near the chest. The only identifier that tells you this jacket belonged to Merton is the number inside: 127. This laundry number is how the monks would get the right clothing back after the washing had been done. Two numbers above the 127 have been crossed out with a marker, indicating the jacket had two owners previous to Merton—owners who had either left the monastery or died. The lining—striped in dark gray, peach, purple, and light blue—made it suitable for cold-weather wear.

There are photos of him wearing it, his hands in the pockets to protect them from the cold. Merton owned this one jacket and no other.

The jacket and other items Merton personally owned were only discovered in 2015 by a Missouri writer, John Smelcer, who tracked down a rumor he'd heard of an elderly woman who, for some reason, had the famous monk's belongings in her possession. As it turned out, she was a former nun, Helen Marie, who married a monk, Brother Irenaeus, who had been the tailor for Merton's monastery. In fact, the three of them had been friends, and when the monk and nun fell in love, Merton encouraged them to marry. Not long after Merton died, the two left their communities and moved to Kansas City, taking Merton's belongings with them. They did this despite Brother Irenaeus's orders from the abbot of Gethsemani to destroy the items so that they wouldn't become prey for relic hunters.

I'm glad these things survived. There is something to meditate on—the singularity and simplicity of these few items. Other clothing in the stash included two pairs of socks, two knit hats, two pairs of jeans, a dusty and well-worn denim shirt, Merton's scapular (monk's hood), and a hardcover copy of the Psalms, the binding broken and the cover detached from constant use. I consider all these and think of how for you, Thomas, this was enough. You didn't need anything else. I wonder what it would be like to live with so few possessions.

The key seems to be in letting go of what we think we need. When Merton, in 1966, had the opportunity to meet with friends at the Louisville airport, he knew he wasn't attired well. This was the era when people dressed up to fly. However, he didn't allow this to stop him, and he didn't make himself miserable berating himself for how he looked. He focused on his clothing only enough to laugh at himself and instead spent his time enjoying the company. "I had on only my Trappist overalls but anyhow we got into the Luau Room at the airport," he writes. "Lots of rich people were arriving for the [Kentucky] Derby (which is today) and the place was full of brass and money and there I sat having a marvelous time, looking like a convict."

Try to catch yourself wanting something. Ask if there's some other hunger or some poverty of the spirit involved—something deeper that the want cannot fulfill. If you're responding to a commercial and thinking the thing you own is somehow lacking, stop yourself and think about what you do have and in how many ways it is enough. Yes, the new phone has a snazzy professional camera and tons more storage, but your camera takes excellent photos (it may even be why you bought it in the first place), and the amount of storage is fine. You keep your car in good repair, and it gets you where you want to go despite not having a heads-up display and the latest audio technology. That new handbag has lots of pockets, but can you carry what it would take to fill them all?

As Merton writes, we have to exercise this feeling of "enough." But we also have to recognize a certain tension inherent in this sensibility—this isn't about being stingy or coming always from a place of grasping and lack. He observes,

> Knowing when you do not need any more. Acting just enough. Saying enough. Stopping when there is enough. Some may be wasted, nature is prodigal. Harmony is not bought with parsimoniousness.

Yet stopping is "going on." To cling to something and want
more of it, to *use* it more, to squeeze enjoyment out of it. This
is to "stop" and not "go on." But to leave it alone at the right
time, this is the right stopping, the right going on. To leave
a thing alone before you have had anything to do with it, if
it is for your use, to leave it without use, is not "stopping," it
is not even beginning. Use it to go on.

For me, "going on" looks like holding something in love
but being willing to let it go—not because I have to get rid
of it in a flurry of decluttering but because it has to leave my
life when a turn of events warrants it. And knowing that's
OK. I used to think about what I would grab in the event of
a fire in my house. I thought I'd grab two photo albums—the
one containing my wedding photos and the scrapbook docu-
menting the first year of my son's life. My laptop would be
next, and perhaps even the external hard drive I keep on my
desk. But lately I think about how there are old photos, like
ones you might find at a thrift store in old fancy frames, and
how there's no one alive who knows the names or the stories
of the people in the pictures. I rarely look at my old photos.
I could let them go. And so much, including the content
of my computer, is floating around in a digital cloud. The
rest would be replaceable—if I wanted to replace it, which
I may not. Now I believe I would grab, if I could, what has
sentimental value that would help sustain me and that can't
be replaced: The jewelry belonging to my friend Katy, now
deceased, that I wear for speaking engagements. My mother's
Bible and one of her crocheting needles. My father's navy-
blue captain's cap. But if I lost these as well? I would grieve,

but I would use the memory of the love connected to these items to move on.

And I stop coveting by not looking. I don't browse through real estate brochures, though I love looking at houses and apartments. I don't scroll through shopping websites unless I'm looking for something specific. When I'm in Manhattan, the store windows no longer get my prime attention. I ignore the style section of the *New York Times*. I stop coveting by seeing less. There are days when I must close my eyes.

But I can't go through life that way. I know I must think differently so that I can see differently. If I don't, another issue can press in on me—one Merton addresses here:

> We pride ourselves on renouncing the *highest* natural goods, goods which in themselves are spiritual and easily super naturalized and tend to lead us to God. For instance, married love in its most spiritual form—or art, music, scholarship, culture, and all the spiritual pleasures which go with them.
>
> The renunciation of these things is not valid unless we are able to go beyond them and to fill the emptiness caused by their loss—to fill that emptiness with God Himself. Only a really spiritual man is capable of doing this—a highly spiritual man with very spiritual gifts.
>
> But such gifts are very often lacking in contemplatives. They would often be more truly contemplative if they accepted, or even *sought* these goods—I mean art, culture. For in "renouncing" them they often create a void which they fill with something lower—preoccupation with business, or worse still, preoccupation with themselves, with their health, their hurt feelings, etc.

Yes, Thomas, we must be careful. When we remove something from our lives, whether good or bad, it leaves a void. Nature will seek to fill it, sometimes with contempt for others who haven't done the work or who haven't made the choices you have. This will turn to a festering resentment if we don't look to it and constantly remember we are our own instruments of peace through our connection to God. But how do we fill the emptiness with God? I think it comes from developing trust—seeing how God is already dialoguing with us and providing what we ask for. But if we aren't aware of our consciousness, we aren't aware that we already asked for something, let alone that it's already been given.

THE YELLOW CHAISE

Here's what I mean. Several years ago, when I still lived in Manhattan, I became enamored of a chaise lounge I saw for sale in a store that was going out of business down the street from my apartment. I'd never seen a chaise as a piece of indoor furniture, only as a beach or deck chair. I sat on the chaise and—remember my vivid imagination—I wove this whole vision of sitting on that chaise in my home office and reading manuscript pages with a cup of tea by my side. (Note: I didn't have a home office at the time.) That vision felt great, but the price tag on that chaise—about $1,500—was way out of my league, especially, in practical terms, for a frivolous piece I didn't need.

A few weeks later, my husband and I were in a neighborhood thrift store shopping for shirts. While he perused the racks, I went to sit down, and guess what I found in the second-hand furniture section? A chaise. The white twill cover was dingy and the cushions thin, but I could afford it: $225. I thought about my vision and what it would be like to have a house of my own with that home office. But then this thought came to me, loud and clear: *This is not my chaise.*

I didn't tell anyone about my very odd desire, not even my husband, because it all seemed, well, silly. In those days, my prayers to God weren't about the chaise, but they were about the vision. I had been trying to figure out a way to work from home. My husband and I wanted to start a family, and I knew I wanted to be a mother who was at home, but I still needed to make money. I wasn't sure if that vision was even a possibility. The chaise? I put it down as something I'd buy for myself one day when I hit it big.

Not long after this, I got a phone call from my friend Jenny. She said, "Come over. I have something for you." There was a lot of work going on in her apartment because an interior designer for a major magazine was doing a makeover of Jenny's great room for an upcoming feature. She took me into a room being used for storage, turned on a light, and said, "This is for you. I think you're supposed to have it." There, practically glowing in the center of the room, was a chaise: yellow, slim, with a curved back, tufted fabric, and mahogany legs. It was sleek, smart, and fabulous. I was stunned. I stood there and fought back tears because I just couldn't explain how humbled and loved I felt in that moment. I felt as though God were saying to me, "Anything you want, little girl. *Anything.*" Today it sits in my home office, where I work from home, in the house where we are raising a son.

I haven't wanted anything like that chaise since then, and I think it's because something in me knows I don't have to. I will always have what I need, large or small. And that goes beyond basic needs. Yes, Christ talked about the lilies of the field and how they want for nothing and how God cares for us in the same way. But I think God wants us to have more—not more stuff but more of what's good for us: more of what inspires us and more of what brings us joy. More of what will bring us closer to Creator Spirit. God is aware of the void left when we deny ourselves and would save us from it. Christ came into the world so that we might have life and joy and have it more abundantly. Perhaps the fruit of that abundance is how we fill the void: we fill it with gratitude. We recognize what we already have, and we honor the grace by which we have it. We see, not in order to covet, but to recognize that our cups are full. In fact, they overflow. We don't need anything more. It is enough.

3

Your Work and God's Work

HOW TO PUT AMBITION IN ITS PLACE

Finally, I am coming to the conclusion that my highest ambition is to be what I already am.

NOT LONG AFTER HIS BAPTISM IN THE CATHOLIC CHURCH in November 1938 but before his move to the monastery, Merton moved to a one-room apartment in New York City's Greenwich Village. From a corner mailbox near his apartment, he proceeded to regularly mail submissions of his writing to journals and magazines and publishers. He wrote poems, novels, and book reviews, and everything except the book reviews came back to him with rejection letters. Apparently the failures only spurred him on and made the eager young man even more hungry to publish. He writes, "My chief concern was now to see myself in print. It was as if I could not be quite satisfied that I was real until I could feed my ambition with these trivial glories."

I empathize with this young, ambitious Thomas, especially during the weeks he was waiting to hear about a book he had submitted when he grew impatient to the point where he laments, "I miss my novel." It's been years since publishers required paper manuscripts for submissions, but I can imagine what it must have been like for him to be full of hope as he sent off that stack of pages.

Yet to say he couldn't be satisfied that he even existed until he saw himself in print? That goes beyond, I think, a writer's usual desire to get work published. Merton wanted more than a book advance and more than his name on the cover of a book. He recognized this: "This was what I really believed in: reputation, success," he writes. "I wanted to live in the eyes and the mouths and the minds of men." So Merton was only in his twenties, and he was already thinking about fame, about awards, about legacy.

Again, I don't blame him, because I'm thinking of his manuscripts. So many writers spend their days in front of blank screens and blank pages, filling the void with thousands of words that have no guarantee of being read. Some are fine with that and will tell you their writing is an end in itself and doesn't have to go beyond their own desk. But I have no interest in being Emily Dickinson, scribbling obscurely on the backs of envelopes, or Charlotte Brontë submitting her *Jane Eyre* under the pseudonym of Currer Bell. If I have put my heart and soul into a piece of writing, then letting people know about it is, to me, the obvious next step. I'm not sure the writing has served its purpose if it's not acknowledged.

Is it wrong to want something, even if it's as bold and vain as Merton describes, out of all that work? The answer, as the young Merton figured, was both no and yes.

He writes, "How could I love God when everything I did was done not for Him but for myself, and not trusting in His aid, but relying on my own wisdom and talents?" In other words, it was fine to want to be a good writer and to want to be published. It was not so great to have this focus be only for his own end, his own personal glory. And yet most egos want, even need, to be fed. How are we to reconcile this, especially when we are raised in a society that cultivates ambition? From our earliest days at school, we are meant to strive for the best grades in the classroom, the best performances onstage and on the sports fields, and then to get into the best colleges, to aim for the best jobs, and to rise to the highest possible positions. When someone isn't considered ambitious, they are seen as lacking—no willingness to go for the jugular.

But Merton, though young, was awake enough to know when pride and ambition drove his actions and aware enough to know what was missing: God. He had God-given gifts, and yet he had been determined to use those gifts as he saw fit to attain the very ego-driven goals he wanted: the satisfaction of seeing his name in print, the hope that his name would live on when others had been forgotten, some notoriety that would allow him to stand a little taller at the next party when talking to the next pretty girl he wanted to impress. He writes, "Of course, as far as my ambitions went, their objects were all right in themselves. There is nothing wrong in being a writer or a poet—at least I hope there is not: but the harm lies in wanting to be one for the gratification of one's own ambitions, and merely in order to bring oneself up to the level demanded by his own internal self-idolatry."

We all have gifts, but we often make our own decisions on how these gifts are to be used and valued with no thought as to how they are meant to play a role in God's creation. For all we know, God means for us to play a bigger game, one that could serve our ambitions as well as God's plans. But we get in our own way with our own notions of success.

Even the monk-to-be Merton thought he knew the best way to serve God and tamp down his puffed-up ambitions—stop being a writer altogether. Before leaving New York for the Abbey of Gethsemani in Kentucky, Merton, in addition to disposing of his belongings, burned three manuscripts of novels he'd written. He thought he was starting a life of prayer and contemplation, a life that wouldn't involve wrestling words onto a page.

But if this were truly the case, what do we make of the fact that he didn't burn everything? He sent his poems and two journals to friends, though he doesn't say whether he sent these pages for possible publication or for safekeeping. Then once he was at the monastery and waiting in his room for further direction, how did he occupy himself? He worked on a poem he intended for a farewell for a couple of his friends. He couldn't stop writing in the same way he couldn't stop breathing. The monk who finally summoned him "hid his face behind his hands to laugh when I told him what I was doing. 'A *poem*?' he said, and hastened out of the room." This was probably his first inkling that, he writes, "there was this shadow, this double, this writer who had followed me into the cloister."

THE STRUGGLE

Brother Louis (the monastic name given to Merton) soon learned this "double" was a force to be reckoned with:

> He rides my shoulders, sometimes, like the old man of the sea. I cannot lose him. He still wears the name of Thomas Merton . . . he meets me in the doorway of all my prayers, and follows me into church. He kneels with me behind the pillar, the Judas, and talks to me all the time in my ear. He is a business man. He is full of ideas. He breathes notions and new schemes. He generates books in the silence that ought to be sweet with the infinitely productive darkness of contemplation. And the worst of it is, he has my superiors on his side. They won't kick him out. I can't get rid of him.

Indeed, when Merton first spoke to his superiors about his writing, he did so as a kind of confession, as something he felt he would give up so he could clear his path to prayer. To his surprise, Dom Frederic, then the head of the abbey, had a different idea: "[He] decided that I should write books. It was he who firmly and kindly encouraged me and indeed ordered me to continue, in spite of my own misgivings." Merton had misgivings because he knew the size of his ego and how perfectly capable it was of becoming a ravenous and ambitious monster. Thus began his struggle to successfully do the work he was meant to do while keeping this monster at bay.

But Thomas, I wonder, Is it wise to starve the monster even as you're holding it off? If you don't allow it small pleasures, won't it become more insistent on having its own way? You write often of holding back and "writing carefully and well for the glory of God, denying myself, and checking my haste to get into print." And this even as the page proofs came in for *The Seven Storey Mountain*: "As usual I have to check my appetite for books and work and keep close to God in prayer. Which is what He wants." Once the book came out, you even worried about taking too much pleasure in the publication and having the kind of daydreams that can follow such an achievement: "I caught myself thinking, 'If they make it into a movie, will Gary Cooper be the hero?' . . . But anyway that is the kind of folly I have to look out for now."

THE MONSTER REARS UP

So no folly. No daydreams. Just work and more work. Writing and more writing. Don't feed the monster. At some point, Merton must have understood that he was only provoking these aspects in himself by trying to deny them. When we don't make peace with or understand ambition, the monster, full of pride and resentment, rears up and makes life messy. "We do not know how to do things well," he writes. "We concentrate so much that we get ourselves mixed up and we make so many dumb plans that God can't do anything with us." In the ensuing years, Merton would publish *The Seven Storey Mountain* and become famous in a way he couldn't enjoy in the secular world. He couldn't do book signings or speaking engagements. The only difference for him was that more of his work was wanted, so he kept producing—at least a dozen books and scores of essays, articles, and reviews. And of course poems. On top of this, he was named master of novices in 1955, adding to his work a substantial amount of teaching and the preparation it required. He became so busy that there are breaks in his journaling for months at a time.

But the monster has done all this work. He must have something to show for it, if only admiration. Merton felt this, much to his chagrin: "Someone accused me of being a 'high priest' of creativity. Or at least of allowing people to regard me as one. This is perhaps true. The sin of *wanting to be a pontiff*, of wanting to be heard, of wanting converts, disciples. Being in a cloister, I thought I did not want this. Of course I did and everyone knows it."

Not long after making this admission, Merton was approached by an editor to assemble an anthology of his writing into a book that eventually became *A Merton Reader*. He leapt at the chance, intrigued by the notion that he could have such a book and that his writing was at a level that warranted the recognition. But even as he worked on the volume, he writes,

It brought me again into the realm of doubt and uncertainty. It seems to be necessary and right and then at moments I glimpse all the possibilities of dishonesty and self-deception it brings with it. The creation of another image of myself—fixation on the idea that I am a "writer who has arrived"—which I am. But what does it mean? Arrived where? Void. Has there been anything else in my life but the construction of this immense illusion? And the guilt that goes with it, what is this? A justification for it, a second illusion? Certainly I can have no peace in this kind of nonsense.

What made matters worse was the fact that working on the book made Merton realize he'd been so intent on publishing wherever and whenever he could that his professional life was in great disorder. Without realizing it, he had violated contracts with different publishers, agreeing to write for one, for example, when his next work was promised to another. One dispute nearly erupted into a lawsuit from Macmillan and caused friction for Merton with his friend Bob Giroux, who published Merton at Farrar, Straus and Giroux. A few publishers wouldn't allow material from their Merton books to be reprinted in *A Merton Reader*. Merton blamed it all on his ambition: "The root of the trouble was my own impatience to get the *Reader* done, and that was nothing but self-love and ambition, unworthy of a monk."

But really, the unfed monster must be acknowledged. Merton's overwork—his ridiculous level of productivity—led to the kind of acting out that strong emotions require. I know the hunger for recognition and attention to my work, and I know the emotions. More than a year after I graduated with my MFA degree, I still hadn't sold my next novel. I had no job. I carried the manuscript around in a binder, like a child I didn't want to leave alone, as proof I hadn't wasted the previous four years. But after another set of rejection letters, when the pain got to be too much, I prayed with one simple message: I was angry.

I had felt ignored, passed over, disrespected, and lost in a void where I had no way of knowing what was to come next. I looked at opportunities with skepticism. I'd received such a weird, haphazard inquiry from an organization that it made me think they were only asking for me because they couldn't get someone else. In another moment, I learned my payment hadn't been processed for a gig I'd done weeks before. I felt tired and broke.

But I also realized my anger was really about my monster—my ego. I kept opening my email to learn of awards, residencies, jobs I had not received. I was frustrated about the time it had taken me to apply for these things, and now I had nothing to show for it. My social media was filled with announcements from the writers who'd encountered just the opposite. I wanted to do big things. I wanted my work to be recognized and rewarded. But was I, with these desires, somehow getting in my own way? Is it possible to be ambitious and humble? Can my work and God's work coexist?

It seemed the best Merton could do was police his selfish, egotistical impulses with a huge dose of guilt. He berated himself whenever he gave rein to prideand feeling special. I find it interesting that he says in this journal entry that he doesn't know where his problems spring from. And yet it's obvious he knows exactly where he strays off course, especially when it comes to mean-spirited thinking. "All day I have been uncomfortably aware of the wrong that is in me," he writes. "The useless burden of pride I condemn myself to carry—and all that comes with carrying it. I know I deceive myself, as a monk and as a writer. But I do not see exactly where. Trying to do things that are beyond me, no doubt. Trying to have something to say about everything. Not enough mistrust of my own opinion. And beyond that, a rebellious and nasty dissatisfaction with things, with the country, the Church."

WHAT PLEASES YOU

The heart of Merton's issues with ambition, I believe, goes back to his notion of there being two versions of himself: the monk Brother Louis, on the one hand, and the Thomas Merton who sneaked into the monastery with him, on the other. Whenever we split ourselves, there will be problems. It's like that popular advice about lying: if you don't lie, then you won't have to remember what you told to whom. It's a wholeness issue. If you have to remember all your different lies, then you're presenting a different person to different people depending on what lie you've told. You've split yourself, and the division drains your brain, exhausted from trying to reconcile the separate parts. In battling his ego, it was inevitable Merton would eventually recognize that the monster was only himself, and he had to be reconciled to it. He writes, "I will never fulfill my obligation to surpass myself unless I first accept myself—and if I accept myself fully in the right way I will already have surpassed myself. For it is the unaccepted self that stands in my way—and will continue to do so as long as it is not accepted. When it has been accepted—it is my own stepping stone to what is above me."

Perhaps the acceptance is in allowing, not limiting, ourselves to do what we want. Like Merton allowing himself to write and enjoy it, for example, because he was someone who read a lot and had a lot of things to say. But because he knew he wanted a lot of other things from writing—recognition, legacy, even love—he held onto the work in an unhealthy way. Ambition can make us grasp, with white knuckles and grim determination, the thing that we think will bring us the success we want. I feel sorry for college students who think they have to know exactly what they're going to major in and then what kind of job they will have after school. Once they think they have an answer, they hold on to this thing they think they want to be, like a kid who always said he wanted to be a doctor or a lawyer when he was in fifth grade. He pushes himself through medical school or law school and becomes that successful doctor or lawyer and then doesn't know how to let it all go when he doesn't like what he does, especially if his family insists he hold on. Ambition can push us to a place where we can't enjoy our work. It might be the evil distorting what God wants for us.

When the author Barbara Brown Taylor was a seminary student, she thought she needed to know exactly what she was going to do when she graduated because her classmates had such crystal-clear notions of their callings. After much prayer, she sensed this response: "Do anything that pleases you, and belong to me." The answer left her surprised and confused but, on a certain level, I think, also relieved. She eventually came to realize, "It was not *what* I did but *how* I did it that mattered."

Once, in a workshop with the speaker and author Rob Bell, he asked me why I write. I said it was like asking me why I had an arm. I've been writing since I was a child. As we spoke and I thought more about what my childhood writing had been like, I recalled that I hadn't been concerned about awards and residencies and publication. I put words on the page because

I enjoyed it and I felt so like myself when I did it. He reminded
✔ me that writing as a child had been play for me and should
continue to be so. I wanted to laugh, because a friend once
told me I worked too hard and I only needed to trust what I
did and continue doing it. "Don't you realize you are like Harry
Potter?" she said. "You need to respect your magic."

I have to admit, whenever I have prayed about what to
do, the answer to my prayers has always been "Just write." I
keep getting knocked upside the head with this message, and
now here it was again from Rob Bell. I think my way of being
humble would be to finally listen to the message and tell my
ego to shut up.

WHEN WORK FEELS LIKE JOY

I'm thinking about what it would look like to, as my friend sug-
gested, respect my magic. I'm not sure it would be like playing
exactly, but I do have a sense of the feeling—like Eric Liddell
running. I'm thinking of the film *Chariots of Fire*, about Liddell, a Christian missionary and a talented runner from Scot-
land who won a gold medal in the 1924 Summer Olympics.
There's a scene in which he's late to a prayer service because
he'd been training for the Olympics, and he is chastised by his
sister, who fears his growing popularity and focus on running
are drawing his attention away from their religious work. She's
especially worried he will be overtaken by pride and ego. But
he insists that isn't what running is for him. He believes it is his
God-given talent. "God made me fast," he says. "When I run, I
feel His pleasure." And indeed you see him begin a race with

his torso straight upright, his legs pumping in the disciplined rhythm of a sprinter. But as his speed increases and he leaves his competitors in the dust, a kind of release occurs. His chin lifts, his head is thrown backward, and his arms windmill out in sheer ecstasy.

There is divine connection and joy and light. And if Merton could have reveled in his gifts, he may have felt something similar. Perhaps Merton did taste a bit of this joy. There's a Merton quote that shows up in a lot of compendiums, but I can't find its original source. It says, "When ambition ends, happiness begins." I think letting go of ego and doing what we do best because it's simply what we do seems like a good way to be.

When I think of how much Merton wrote—some say compulsively—and how many books, letters, articles, and poems he produced, I realize this may have been his manner of windmilling his way through the use of his God-given gift. But Merton's ego wouldn't allow him to reach and enjoy the levels of Liddell's ecstasy. However, he did appreciate knowing that when he was aligned with his gift, he could affect people in a positive way. On receiving letters from readers of *Seven Storey Mountain* describing how much the book helped them, Merton writes, "I love the people who say this, because they are sincere and because they are after all giving glory to God and not to me. The letters they write are mostly about God and about their rediscovery of a thing called hope, which almost seems to have died in the world they live in. This much is serious. But I do not have to delude myself that because they love God I am somehow important."

I'm stunned by how low-key he sounds about their rediscovery of "a thing called hope." I wish Merton could have taken this piece to help him understand that at the end of the day, his writing wasn't about him. It was about "a thing called hope," and it was about faith, and it was about God and love and so many of the ideas and feelings and dreams that, when stitched together, allow people to create a picture that makes sense of their lives.

I'm guessing that in your prayerful moments, Thomas, you realized helping people was what your work was really about. Maybe this knowledge is what inspired you to keep going. By the time you published *A Merton Reader*, it seemed you were ready to let go, at least a bit, of wanting your writing to be anything more than it was. I think of you with empty hands because you've given away the best of who you were. I hope you became lighter for it.

"In religious terms, this is simply a matter of accepting life, and everything in life as a gift, and clinging to none of it, as far as you are able," you write. "You give some of it to others, if you can. Yet one should be able to share things with others without bothering too much about how they like it, either, or how they accept it. Assume they will accept it, if they need it. And if they don't need it, why should they accept it? That is their business. Let me accept what is mine and give them all their share, and go my way."

4

I Am a Bird, Waiting

HOW TO FIND GOD'S PRESENCE IN NATURE

One bird sits still
Watching the work of God.

OVER THE COURSE OF A WET AND CHILLY WEEKEND IN December, I walked in the footsteps of Thomas Merton. I wouldn't call my trip to his corner of Kentucky a pilgrimage. I knew I would do some praying when I joined the monks in their daily cycle of chanting and prayer, but I didn't have a plan beyond that. I'd traveled alone, and I wasn't sure how comfortable I'd be rambling the woods by myself. But I knew I wanted to try.

The grounds of the Abbey of Gethsemani cover nearly 1,500 acres of hills (called "knobs"), valleys, lakes, fields, and forests. To know Merton's work is to know this landscape, because he photographed it and wrote about it so often: from basic observations about the weather to contemplative ruminations connecting the natural world to the divine presence at work. His observant eyes and ears absorbed the vital details, and he found words to bring it all to life. Such words from his book

Conjectures of a Guilty Bystander are what first captivated me, as I heard out loud his descriptions of birdsong awakening, each in their own turn. Even now when I hear a crow, I think of how he thought, "The waking of crows is most like the waking of men: querulous, noisy, raw."

Merton's connection with this corner of the earth, located fifty miles south of Louisville, Kentucky, is so deeply personal. It only made sense for me to venture out and, in a fashion, meet him where he once was. I pulled on my hiking boots and zipped up my coat. I studied the map on the sheet of paper I received from the lobby desk of the abbey's guesthouse and then set out down the driveway under a tin-gray sky.

I assumed Merton's connection to the woods around the monastery grew from his earliest days as a young novice. While there is some truth to that, Merton's direct experience of the land came much later. The property behind the abbey's church and the monastery itself are walled-off enclosures. When Merton first arrived at Gethsemani, monks were not allowed outside the walls except for work assignments such as clearing brush in the fields or planting trees in the woods. His days were spent in cycles of prayer, study, and writing. Even today on the monastery's website, a note to visitors reads, "We ask you to bear in mind that the monastic life is lived as a separation from the world."

Merton lived the first eight years of his monastic life for the most part behind the abbey's walls. And yet he found the experience less than peaceful. He chafed at having little time to himself because of his duties, and as royalties from his books flowed and the abbey began the noisy work of renovations and the mechanization of its farming and cheese-making activities, he found quiet hard to come by as well. He wanted solitude.

He thought about leaving for a different monastic order, the Camaldolese, in which the monks lived in solitude as hermits. His superiors tried to assuage his desire to leave by allowing him solitary spaces for his writing and reading. But then, unexpectedly, about a month after his ordination to the priesthood, Merton writes that on June 27, 1949, "Reverend Father . . . gave me permission to go out of the enclosure into the woods by myself."

On that day, his writing and his spirituality changed forever. This footnote appears on the page of that day's journal entry: "The expansiveness and depth of Merton's prose, as he recalls his walk, marks June 27, 1949, as a day on which Merton's life at Gethsemani breaks out beyond a past mental and physical confinement." In the book *Thomas Merton's Gethsemani: Landscapes of Paradise*, author Monica Weis notes of this time, "Once beyond the monastery walls, Merton's heart soared."

TUNING IN

I figured it would be easy enough to make it to St. Edmond's Lake, less than half a mile from the abbey and, according to my map, pretty much a straight shot once I crossed the road, Highway 247. I could be back in less than an hour, in time for the None prayer at 2:15 p.m. The path took me through harvested fields that rolled up and away from me to my right. I wondered if these were the same fields that Merton had worked as a young man, before the abbey had machinery to tend the farm. He had relished the exertion of harvesting corn and cutting tobacco, and he enjoyed the fellowship of his monastery brothers toiling with him under the sun. Three or four grand old trees stood out in the distance, rising up from the fields with their bare branches and straight trunks. They reminded me of the tree in the field Red (Morgan Freeman) is looking for when he seeks out Andy's (Tim Robbins) gift for him at the end of the film *The Shawshank Redemption*. I stepped around muddy puddles left from an earlier pouring rain.

It's a known fact that going outside and being in nature is good for us. But what Merton experienced that first day of being allowed outside the walls and on the days that followed was beyond taking a hike and beyond simply stopping to smell the roses. Merton's heart didn't soar, profoundly touched, because he took a walk. He felt something out there—something I daresay so many of us seek when we are hungering for an experience of God. "As soon as I get away from people the Presence of God invades me," he writes. "And when I am not divided by being with strangers (in a sense anyone I live with will always remain a stranger), I am with Christ." Merton found somehow beneath the branches, on the sides of the hills, in all of nature a sense of transcendence. I'm guessing that after being doused in words for so many years, suddenly he could be in this expansive, silent space with God and just listen. This was not necessarily prayer, which people usually understand to be about talking to God. This was about reaching out. This was about feeling. Within the monastery walls, it was as if he were continually fussing with the dials of an old ham radio, hoping to tune into a divine frequency. But outside? He could be the antennae. Maybe even be the frequency.

To me, this is transcendence—which, as Thomas has helped me understand, is about an awareness, perhaps even a fine tuning. I'm not sure there are even proper words for what I'm trying to describe. It looks like a complete oneness with all of creation. Since my baptism in 2011 in the Episcopal Church, I've often thought about that oneness and about what belonging to Christ means. From my observations, it seems this is expressed in terms of action—what one does, how one behaves. Love others, do good works, live into charity, mercy, and forbearance. But there's a shift within as well. I feel it as a release of ego and my very essence. What Thomas describes is the feeling when I do so. When I can make this release, it puts me in the same room with the divine.

How can we use nature to cultivate an awareness of God? How do we enter a space of reverence, where there are no walls and no ceilings and yet where we find a room we share with Creator Spirit? Merton had pondered this as well that first day walking in the forest: "And I thought: If we only knew how to *use* this space and this area of sky and these free woods."

Considering his reflections on that pivotal day and then how he lived and wrote afterward, I think the answer to this cultivation question comes in three pieces. He began by going out every day and walking the earth in a sacred manner—meaning reverently, with his whole being open to the feel of the earth underneath him and of the air around him. Merton often walked barefoot so that he could better appreciate connecting with the ground. The second piece involved an

ongoing acknowledgment of the weather. The third seemed
to be about learning all he could about the "rooms" of his
outdoor home, including the names of the flowers and trees
that furnished it and the birds and animals who resided there.
The assembled wisdom of these pieces brought Merton to the
unity of creation and his place in it: "How absolutely central
is the truth that we are first of all *part of nature*, though we
are a very special part, that which is conscious of God. In
solitude, one is entirely surrounded by beings which perfectly
obey God."

Merton's words make me smile. It's like he recognizes a
different monastery existing on the property of Gethsemani.
He knew there would be much to learn there, and he was
eager to do so.

REVERENCE AND THE GIVING OF THE SELF

The vegetation at the edge of St. Edmond's Lake was all brown
and tired looking. There were a few evergreens, but they were
on the sides farthest from where I was. The lake was quite still,
reflecting the trees all around it. The scene was not necessarily
pretty or inspiring.

Because I'd reached my destination and also because it
was cold outside, there was every reason for me to turn back
and return to the abbey as I'd planned. But I didn't move. I
felt entranced by something I heard, and that sensation was
holding me there.

My son is a Boy Scout, so I know all about being prepared
and having maps and compasses and water and a good plan

for a hike. But they don't talk about what can happen if the landscape takes hold of your spirit. From Merton's experience, it seems that when you go out in search of spirit, you begin by walking the earth with reverence, as though your whole body is one great ear and you are listening. So you have to be prepared when the earth grabs your ear so you can receive an answer. Are you willing to give in to the tug when you feel it? When I do, I sense I have to give myself to the space, in terms of understanding it and also my humanity within it.

I'm not sure how to explain this other than to say that when we are in nature's space, something about it may capture us to the point that if we had concerns about the outing, they all fall away. On Merton's first outing, the concern had been lightning, but in his captivation by his surroundings, that concern evaporated: "The Spirit of God got hold of me. . . . I used to be afraid of lightning before I came to the monastery. Now there didn't seem to be any particular objection to walking right into the storm although behind me was the big field where two boys were killed by lightning last summer or the one before."

I'm not saying one doesn't practice safety and take precautions—a charged-up cell phone and proper cold-weather gear, for instance. I know I wasn't sure I'd feel safe hiking all by myself in unknown territory. That's why I had planned to stay close to the abbey.

But as I said before, this thing had a hold on me. It was silence.

I have no doubt it was the same silence that Merton, enthralled with what he'd heard on his first walk, had called

✓ "the marvelous quiet!" I heard it, Thomas. And it was indeed so stunning that I could only marvel. It was amazing: how I could be standing in such a big open space, sky all around me, and have it be filled with a lovely silence. I heard a few notes of birdsong in the distance, but it was still so quiet—a beautiful, comforting, engulfing silence. I was so struck by it that I even tried to capture it in a video. But I kept thinking, "This was what Thomas loved."

✓ I walked a little farther. The woods felt encompassing and healing despite it being the dead of winter with few signs of life to be found. I realized I had a decision to make. I could keep to my schedule and return to the abbey, or I could give in to this silence.

I looked at my map. The trail leading deep into the woods was marked by numbered signposts. As long as I was careful to stay on it, I wouldn't get lost. I thought about the upcoming None prayer, but I already knew I would ignore the church bells. I didn't know how far I was going, and it didn't matter—I had surrendered to whatever would come next.

Connecting to divine spirit requires surrender. Giving myself over to the silence meant I would surrender control of my footsteps, my plans, and all expectations. I wasn't afraid. When my hands weren't cold, I walked with them at my side, my palms open. "Again, sense of the importance, the urgency of seeing, fully aware, experiencing what is *here*: not what is given by men, by society, but what is given by God and hidden by (even monastic) society," writes Merton. "Clear realization that I must begin with these first elements. That it is absurd to inquire after my function in the world, or whether I have one, as long as I am not first of all alive and awake. And if that, and no more, is my job (for it is certainly every man's job), then I am grateful for it."

I think it was easier for me to give in to the silence because I have been alive and awake to it before. One summer afternoon, I lay on the long, cushioned window seat in our family room and fell asleep. I didn't intend to nap. I'd been sitting there reading and looking out over my lilac bushes and down the road. But at some point, the warmth of the day and the tiredness from a busy week dropped over me, and I closed my eyes. When I awoke, I heard only silence. Not even birds. I recognized this quiet too. Just as there are recognizable voices, there are certain kinds of quietude. Sometimes I think that quiet, the voice of a summer afternoon draped in a light wind and the sound of my own breath, is what God might sound like.

I first heard this voice during the summers of my childhood. Back then, the sound included the playback announcers of the Cleveland Indians baseball game my daddy would be watching on television. Somewhere between the crack of a bat and the notes of the stadium organ, I'd fall asleep. Someone, most likely my eldest brother, would, at Daddy's suggestion, pick me up and put me on the bed to finish my nap in the room I shared with my sisters. When I woke up, I felt this same disinclination to move. I'd gaze at the dust motes floating through the shaft of sunlight beaming through the curtains. I'd listen. Maybe the ball game was still on, but mainly I was listening to the quiet. It fascinated me.

I know some have said God speaks in thunder and lightning, that God is loud and commanding. But I think when God speaks, there is nothing more than quiet and nothing deeper—just the moment, the now. This quiet, then and in the moment walking into the woods of Gethsemani, makes me feel like I'm held in the palm of a hand. It's why I didn't feel afraid. Instead, I kept listening. And I kept walking.

THE WEATHER OF THE WORLD

Merton understood that being tuned into the weather is more than wearing a jacket because it's cold or taking an umbrella because it threatens to rain. It is earth's personality speaking to us, either drawing us in or pressing us away. We already know this on a certain level. How many times have we heard someone say they know rain is coming because their joints ache? But can we bring ourselves to be always listening, to embrace and truly live in the weather of the world?

How you sense the weather's message depends on how your own inner radar works. I can tell you that for me, a December day labeled "unseasonably warm" can have a sepia-toned cloudy sky and a humidity with a kind of softness that makes me want to step inside of it and wrap it around my shoulders. I try to stay outside as much as possible on a day like that. A full moon, subzero-degree night in February can have its own allure that makes me want to learn the constellations and savor the crisp hollow caused by the cold air in the back of my throat. Each aspect of weather nudges me out of my complacency and says, "Look! You are here. Pay attention to the earth turning."

Merton paid close attention and often began his journal entries with weather observations:

Brilliant afternoon. It is the day when everything finally opens out and the green woods on the hills turns definitely into foliage.

Well, another torrent of Rain.

Weather hot as midsummer.

A brilliant Saturday. Bright sky and clouds. Not too hot.

Cold wind and a little snow, the wind making one feel the silence after noon.

Very cold morning, about 8 above zero.

I think we take our weather knowledge for granted. We have the Weather Channel delivering forecasts around the clock, and we carry apps on our phones that can call up radar images at the touch of a screen. I'm friends with one of our local meteorologists, Gil Simmons, and yes, I tune into his forecasts every morning both on television and in his social media videos. But I appreciate that Merton calls us back to a deeper, more convivial relationship with atmospheric conditions. Instead of something to be constantly preparing for, the weather can be something we welcome as a chance to learn about ourselves:

Our mentioning of the weather—our perfunctory observations on what kind of day it is, are perhaps not idle. Perhaps we have a deep and legitimate need to know in our entire being what the day is like, to *see* it and *feel* it, to know how the sky is grey, paler in the south, with patches of blue in the southwest, with snow on the ground, the thermometer at 18, and cold wind making your ears ache. I have a real need to know these things because I myself am part of the weather and part of the climate and part of the place, and a day in which I have not shared truly in all this is no day at all. It is certainly part of my life of prayer.

I feel closest to the earth after the rain. The ground is so soft, and as I walk it, I have this sense of coming home—like I want to lie down in the forest after a warm spring rain, only instead of lying on the earth, I have become the earth, alive and wet and teeming. Flowers could germinate beneath me and grow roots and tendrils through my body until they come from my skin and bloom and bloom and bloom through my mouth and from every square inch of my being. The feeling is exhilarating and devastating. Sublime.

THE NAMES OF THINGS

Once we know the ground beneath our feet and have some understanding of the movement and work of the atmosphere around us, it's time to know the names and habits of those with whom we're sharing the outdoors. Of course, there's a certain folly here. If we're seeking true communion with nature, it would be good to admit the names we learn for plants and animals aren't the names they have for themselves. For all of Merton's close observation of deer near his hermitage, he knew they wouldn't respond if he stood on his porch calling out, "Deer! Hey, deer!" anymore than he would respond if he heard someone calling, "Hey, George!" But since we can never know what the beings of nature call themselves, we have to be content with learning the names we've given them. And we can also know their habits of existing in the world.

Merton used guidebooks to identify the names he didn't know of the birds in the valley, but he had to use his own careful listening and observations to know that they don't all awaken at the same time. He knew the name of "bullfrog," but he also recognized the sedate nature of the amphibian and how the only tone it would offer is "Om." In his journals, he tended to mention not only the plant or bird or animal. He would say something of its nature, which can offer more for us and for him. For example, this: "When I thought the gardenias were all done I found a splendid one this morning in the dark with a flashlight. It budded yesterday afternoon in the rainstorm while I was writing up mystical theology notes." He doesn't just say he saw a gardenia. We learn that it was an unusual find because it's past the time when the other gardenias have all bloomed. We also learn other unusual circumstances—Merton saw it in the dark, and the flower had bloomed in less-than-ideal conditions. Therefore, we can take from it a lesson of beauty and resilience.

In this entry, we get the landscape of a winter sky, and Merton can identify how much night is left as he assesses the positioning of the planets and the lack of stars: "Pure dark sky with only Moon and planets in it, stars already gone. The moon and Venus over the barns, and Mars far over in the west over the road and the fire tower."

In this, Merton admires the beauty and skilled flying of a bird of prey: "Hawk. First shadow flying down the sunlit trees.

Then the bird overhead, barred tail, spotted wings with sun shining through them. A half circle above the elm, then he seemed to put his wings in his pocket and fly like a bullet into the grove across the field."

I'm not good with constellations, but because I've gardened, I know the names of many flowers. No matter where I am, whether in a neighbor's yard or in the woods or assessing a planted pot on a restaurant patio, I recite flower names in my mind because I don't ever want to forget them: Lenten rose, also known as hellebore; adjuga, vinca, also known as periwinkle; pachysandra, salvia, astilbe, coneflower, cosmos. I don't know the sounds of birds as Thomas did, but I do know that the more brightly colored ones, like the red cardinal, are male, and the females are browner or grayer depending on the species. I also know when I see a male, I should look for the female as well. She is never far behind. I know to look for nests in the branches of my lilac bushes.

Why does knowing names matter? Because once we know the names and the blooming, growing, mating, and feeding habits of the flora and fauna around us, we can harvest a calmness of knowing that nature's rhythm and its cycles continue no matter what. February may still be frigid, and my body may be tired from my shoulders being hunched up from the cold, but then I see the first robin in a yard. I'm freezing, but I trust the robin—it knows spring is close even if I can't feel it. I'm comforted and I resolve to be patient with the waning winter.

Thomas likewise could recognize the changing nature of the sun and feel the hope of returning spring: "With the new, comes also memory: as if that which was once so fresh in the past (days of discovery when I was 19 or 20) were very

See M's Palace Red carnation

close again, and as if one were beginning to live again from the beginning: one must experience spring like that. A whole new chance! A complete renewal!"

THE VIEW FROM A DISTANCE

Following the signs for Cross Knob, which I decided would be my destination, I met with a steep climb, almost like a wall in front of me. I knew I was still on the path, so I figured there was no place to go but up. Ideally, I would have had a walking stick—the footing was precarious already from the mud. I put my faith in my low center of gravity and kept my hands out in front of me in case I needed to use them to scramble. It was more like a negotiation than a climb—I had to figure out where best to make my next step. Would those tree roots be too slippery? Would I be better off walking in the mud or avoiding it? I managed it, though. Cross Knob has an elevation of about 800 feet. Contrast that with the abbey's, at 570 feet, and you can get a sense of the rise.

When I had reached the top, I sat for a long time overlooking the abbey. The sky had brightened a little. The hill is called Cross Knob because some years back, when Gethsemani replaced the cross topping its church, someone had the idea to haul the old cross up to the top of this knob. All that's left of it now, though, is a pile of decaying wood. The summit is covered with trees, but I still had a clear view of the abbey, framed by bare branches. The monastery and its various outbuildings sat nestled perfectly in the valley. I could also see a ridge on the other side some distance beyond the abbey. Looking out over the abbey from Cross Knob, I think about how you, Thomas, could look at this view and see your whole world, like in a globe in the palm of your hand— the white church, the monastery, the barn. And you knew the importance of grasping it: "Gethsemani looked beautiful from the hill. It made much more sense in its surroundings. We do not realize our own setting and we ought to; it is important to know where you are put on the face of the earth."

I agree. Wherever we live, to be on this planet at all is an extraordinary gift. The best way to show our gratitude is to learn as much as we can about where we live—where we grew up, where we live now—since it's all a part of us. And if we understand, as one would with a plant, the soil in which we've been planted, we can best know how to feed ourselves. We'll know what will help us grow: "If we instinctively seek a paradisiacal and special place on earth, it is because we know in our inmost hearts that the earth was given us in order that we might find meaning, order, truth, and salvation in it. The world is not only a vale of tears. There is joy in it somewhere. Joy is to be sought, for the glory of God."

I stayed out in the woods for over two hours, taking pictures and listening to the sound of my feet walking through leaves. I wondered if and when I could return to this knob again, possibly in different weather, because I'm curious to see what blooms there. I also wondered what aspects of this silence and the earth are now within me and whether it's something I can say Thomas and I share. But even if I don't return, I'm glad I walked beneath these trees. I'm glad I decided to listen to the silence.

5

When Faith Tires

HOW TO REVIVE SPIRIT AFTER AN EPIPHANY

You do not need to know precisely what is happening, or exactly where it is all going. What you need is to recognize the possibilities and challenges offered by the present moment, and to embrace them with courage, faith and hope.

THERE'S A SIGN ON THE CORNER OF FOURTH AND WALNUT in Louisville, Kentucky, commemorating the spot where Thomas Merton, standing in the middle of a shopping district, looked at the people around him and had an epiphany. Up until then, he had seen himself as cut off and separate from the world in his vocation as a cloistered monk. Up until then, he had thought that his connection to God and his writing about that connection were supposed to be his sole purpose and focus. But that mystical moment on March 18, 1958, when he was surrounded by humanity on a street corner, impressed on him his own sense of being human.

He first writes about it roughly in his journal and then expands on it in what would eventually become the book *Conjectures of a Guilty Bystander*:

> I was suddenly overwhelmed with the realization that I loved all those people, that they were mine and I theirs, that we could not be alien to one another even though we were total strangers. It was like waking from a dream of separateness, of spurious self-isolation in a special world, the world of renunciation and supposed holiness. The whole illusion of separate holy existence is a dream.... This sense of liberation from an illusory difference was such a relief and such a joy to me that I almost laughed out loud. . . . I have the immense joy of being *man*, a member of a race in which God Himself became incarnate. As if the sorrows and stupidities of the human condition could overwhelm me, now I realize what we all are. And if only everybody could realize this! But it cannot be explained. There is no way of telling people that they are all walking around shining like the sun.

The moment marked a turning point in Merton's monastic life, the beginning of what's been called his turning "from cloister toward world." The Louisville sign says Merton's "sudden insight . . . led him to redefine his monastic identity with greater involvement in social justice issues."

The words Merton uses in writing of the epiphany have a sense of wonder and joy and love. They are inspiring. And today, you can find them wherever Merton is quoted. Writer Lori Erickson called Merton's moment "one of the most famous revelations in the history of spirituality"; she says the historical marker is "the only one that I know of in the United States that marks a mystical experience."

Fast-forward one year. Merton was again in Louisville. He doesn't say where, but let's assume he was standing in a similar, if not the same, area. This time he had a very different experience. "Was in Louisville Thursday," he writes. "Hated the town. It was hot and stupid. Hated all the advertisements, the interminable attempts to sell you something, the unbearable excess of needless articles and commodities. Everywhere the world oppresses me with a sense of infinite clutter and confusion—and this is what is worldly in the monastery also. Too much of everything."

One year after his Fourth-and-Walnut epiphany, the town has become "hot and stupid." Part of me wants to say, "What the heck, Thomas?" But I also understand.

HOW LONG DOES AN EPIPHANY LAST?

The spiritual road is ever changing. Epiphanies remain, but the shock of them wears off. The year 1959 would find Merton complaining and impatient. I'm not saying this was wrong of him. In fact, it teaches me how to learn and learn again—that I forever have to seek compassion and miracles, transcendence and revelation. That compassion or transcendence or revelation will not be automatically in my heart because it was there a year, a month, or a week ago. And I have to think about—and trust—the process.

Sometimes the process includes faith becoming, well, tired.

In the late 1950s, Merton suffered a time of vocational crisis. He was unhappy with the busyness of the monastery: the ongoing observances and the increased number of postulants, most of whom he, as master of novices, was responsible for developing. More than ever he began to think that solitude was the answer and that it would be best acquired in a different monastery. "Everything in me cries out for solitude and for God alone," he writes. "The feeling is absolutely terrible—the power of an attraction that seems to draw the whole life out of me, to tear out the roots of my soul."

During this time, Merton's friend Ernesto Cardenal, a Nicaraguan priest and poet who was once a novice at Gethsemani, offered Merton the chance to enter a monastery in Cuernavaca, Mexico. Merton, fluent in Spanish and a passionate reader of Latin American writers, felt inspired by the opportunity. He began a conversation with his abbot and a series of correspondence with superiors in Rome to petition for his release from Gethsemani and permission to become a hermit monk in Cuernavaca.

In the introduction to *A Search for Solitude*, the third volume of Merton's journals covering the years 1952–60, editor Lawrence S. Cunningham talks about how, in his own reading of the fourth-century monastic writer John Cassian, he came across the term *acedia*. It's defined as a listlessness or boredom, often connected to spirituality. It was considered a troublesome condition for longtime monks.

Cunningham, quoting Cassian, notes, "The monk begins to feel a 'horror of the place where he is' and 'disgust with his cell.' The same monk begins to 'complain that he is making no progress' and is 'devoid of all spiritual progress.' Finally, he 'sings the praises of monasteries located in other places' and concludes that 'he cannot get any better as long as he stays in his present place.'" Cunningham then says, "I wrote Cassian's words in my journal with the notation: 'an exact description of TM in 1959.'"

In fact, it's eerie to read Cassian's description of a monk's ✓ acedia, written in the fourth century, and then to read this entry from Merton: "I think it is better simply to face the fact that I am not honestly a monk here and that the customary routines will do nothing to make me one and that in order to be more honest (?) I need to go elsewhere. The problem remains an interior one, of course—and conveniently, we don't define too clearly what we mean by 'monks.' It is not the word that matters, but the search for truth. Here, as far as I can tell, I am at the end of the line—as far as my own personal search is concerned."

Acedia seemed to be Merton's main faith struggle, which *acedia* also included wrestling with his ego, chafing at being obedient to the head of his abbey, and wondering what God's will was for him. His emotions ran so high:

> Yesterday I was bitter for a while, growling to myself. "Yes, we have the Holy Ghost all right—in a cage with His wings clipped." But later during the Gospel *"Non turbetur cor vestrum"* [Let your heart not be disturbed] came through into my heart directed especially to me and I remembered there was no need to be bitter or to work, or even to notice what appears to me to be senseless in our life here (the utter stupidity of Pontifical Tierce, for instance—with little brothers standing around like dolls, holding pieces of liturgical

lingerie with which to dress the abbot. Why do we have to play at being bishops and canons all the time?).

One doesn't need to be a monk to experience a bored and tired faith. The acedia may manifest in different ways—frustration, impatience, a lack of compassion—but the struggles with it are the same. Merton's indecision and equivocation show how one can be so stuck in inertia that it's impossible to even decide what to do about it.

Really, at times in his discernment process, Merton became so tiresome. Reading his journals, I sometimes think he sounds like a man who couldn't decide whether or not to leave his wife. At one point, he writes of the necessity of going someplace new:

> I really want to do all I can to get *beyond* the static and meaningless situation in which I now find myself. There is no question that in some way I have to burst out of limitations and find a new level of spiritual existence and that conventional means are not going to be very useful. Whether the answer lies in another country or not is no matter. I really would like to start over again somewhere else—it would feel fresh and clean. No sense in just clinging to what I am accustomed to.

A month later, he's weighing the hardship that might come of a new vocation:

> Is the freedom precious enough to me for me to pay the price of insecurity, hard work, poverty, loss of health, and becoming a displaced person? And all this at the risk of

perhaps not attaining the freedom I hope for? Or shall I be content to be a docile and approved captive, with an easy life, a certain leisure, and the opportunity to engage in verbal rebellion anytime I feel like it? The answer is obvious. If I have stated the things in its correct terms I am really bound to get out—at least try to—from this community. If I am wrong, I hope I will soon come to see it.

Then, only a week later, Merton seems to have talked himself back into the reasons for staying—one of them being that he's simply not interested enough to go:

Perhaps what is upsetting to me is the fear of uncertainty. If the whole business were really serious, that is if my desire to leave here were serious, the certainty would not matter. But the fact is, I must face it—I have no really strong and positive motives for launching out into something completely new. I am just not sufficiently interested in "starting something." And more and more I see the futility, the absurdity, of simply becoming a "parish priest" in some isolated place. . . . And I don't especially want to live in Mexico, as a hermit or otherwise. . . . If I am asked the question—what do I really want to do? It boils down to what I have done for the best afternoons of last week. The long hours of quiet in the woods, reading a little, meditating a lot, walking up and down in the pine needles in bare feet. If what I am looking for is more of that—why not ask for "more of that"?

It seems the best way to work on acedia is at the source—in one's spirit. Otherwise, making a decision wouldn't matter.

Merton, for example, could have headed off to Mexico only to discover he had the same problems, just in a different location. I do think Merton's idea to "burst out of limitations and find a new level of spiritual existence" is what we are all seeking to do. The question is, How can I find a new level of spiritual existence? Merton writes, "There is the level of faith, on which nothing is seen, and yet there peace is evident, and it is no self-delusion to say 'all manner of thing shall be well' because experience has repeatedly proved it. If only faith can survive the choking complications of our judicial and spiritual red tape."

What to do, Thomas, when my faith is so thin and weak I can't feel it in my hands? It helps to think about what a tired faith may need. From your path, it seems these are the essentials: the right food for the journey to nourish it and some form of practice to help faith grow strong again.

FOOD FOR THE JOURNEY

I'm thinking of the story in 1 Kings 19:4–8, in which the prophet Elijah seems ready to give up the ghost, but suddenly there is a jar of water and a cake baked on hot stones. An angel tells him, "Get up and eat, otherwise the journey will be too much for you" (1 Kgs 19:7). I'm thinking about sustenance and whether or not I'm spiritually starving. Not attending church during the pandemic opened a window for me, and I'm sure many others, to consider what feeds faith. Is it in actual bread—communion—which means a return to worship? Is it in independent activities, such as meditation and reading—a version of Merton's solitude? Have I grown weary in a way that requires something more, like a retreat or a pilgrimage?

Maybe I'm thinking of spiritual food in a way that makes sustenance too hard. Merton talks about joy and its ability to lift a clouded faith. He writes of speaking on joy in a monastery meeting: "I think the chief reason why we have so little joy is that we take ourselves too seriously."

I've seen photos of Merton in joy—with his friends laughing, picnicking, even riding in a convertible. I can believe his words, that he understands the importance of joy. Joy is sublime sustenance. Recently, the Dalai Lama and Archbishop Desmond Tutu of South Africa collaborated on a project, a conversation that became *The Book of Joy*. In it, they talk about the nature of joy, the obstacles to joy, the pillars of joy. They talk about joy practices. It is a wonderful book, and I think Merton would have loved it. But really, in some ways the book would have been just as successful if all the pages were blank except for the one featuring the photograph of the Dalai Lama and Archbishop Desmond Tutu, both eighty-something years old, dancing together at the Dalai Lama's birthday party. The archbishop is grooving a wicked shimmy while the Dalai Lama, his hands out with one wrist draped with prayer beads, looks thrilled to keep up with him. To see their joy tells me all I need.

This food can take us far. It grows from knowing and trusting our connection with God. I believe God's presence is a joyful presence. We just have to allow ourselves to feel it. We have to believe ourselves worthy. Merton gleaned this in his reading of Karl Barth: "Always the old trouble, that the devil and our nature try to persuade us that before we can begin to believe we must be perfect in everything. Faith is not important as it is 'in us.' Our faith is 'in God,' and with even a very little of it, God is in us."

PRACTICING FAITH BECAUSE I'LL NEVER GET IT RIGHT

Practicing faith was, of course, Merton's business as a monk. He was in prayer, worship, and meditation around the clock. And yet this type of intense practice may have contributed to his acedia in the first place. I suppose the question is how to practice fruitfully without succumbing to busyness, which can lead, as it did for Merton, to a kind of disconnect.

In my own busyness, I know I sometimes stray too far from the sound of my Lord's voice. I have to remind myself to take time to listen. When I hit spiritual bumps in the road, maybe the best thing for me is to sit quietly on a cushion at my meditation space and light a candle. I believe reconnecting with a spiritual practice can aid my attitude, but sometimes I feel I need a moment shot through with intense love and joy. Can a spiritual practice do that? Maybe I should read all of Isaiah? Or take up a language? If I study Italian, what will I become? Our habits are our lives.

Merton looked to his own practice for relief, especially when, in December 1959, he received the official "no" from Rome that he couldn't go to another monastery. He had to stay at Gethsemani because, his superiors noted, it was God's will that he do so. Instead of getting angry, Merton began to follow through on an observation he'd made the previous year. "I honestly begin to wonder whether my being bound by vows to this situation is not in some way a great mistake," he writes. "Not that I want to be dispensed from my vows; but I can at least hope for some relief, under the vows themselves. Perhaps this hope is a vain one. . . . Anyway I feel terribly like a prisoner. And the only solution is to do things they do to keep sane in prisons: to follow faithfully my own routine and salvage what I can of my inner liberty."

What if we are all doing this, Thomas? What if the world itself feels like a prison? What if we are walled into our lives and survive only insofar as we can construct that inner liberty? I think of Mick, the girl heroine in Carson McCullers's novel *The Heart Is a Lonely Hunter*. She speaks of furnishing her "inside room," a room within her in which her artistic life and spirit are affirmed. In this room she places Mozart, the pursuit of beauty, the dream of traveling to foreign lands, and the faith that she can create things and loom large because she knows how much her heart swells when she encounters what inspires her.

I think I try to build this room on the foundation of routine, but my routine suffers all sorts of variations, as did Merton's, especially when he had unexpected visitors. He writes of chasing away the people who came upon him at his hermitage as he sat on his porch on a hot day, reading outdoors in his underwear. Also the times he returned from a walk to find visitors waiting, and he hid until they went away. But of course, he liked having the ability to see visitors. He was probably the most popular hermit ever known! He was fiercely independent and somewhat spoiled by always being able, both before becoming a monk and after, to do mostly what he liked. He received visitors, had picnics with friends, and even checked out a jazz club in Louisville. In many ways, one of the reasons he was reluctant to leave Gethsemani was that the monastery offered an order to his life that he could lean into when his thoughts were particularly chaotic.

My routine is about three things: *Pray. Exercise. Write.* If I can do these three things most days of my life, I know, as the Queen song goes, "I should be doing all right." Maybe even more—I can live with freedom and intentionality. As Merton writes, "I will follow my conscience—and my vows—and the Holy Spirit and not expect anybody else in the world to think for me and live my life for me." I guess you could say practice puts meat on the bones of one's faith. The freedom and intentionality come of being stronger in faith, and in this strength, the apathy and listlessness of acedia can only fade.

A FAITH REVIVED

Once a faith has been properly nourished and revived, what does it look like? What does it feel like? Light! That's the best way I can describe it. A feeling of light within me, all around me. Just light. In Merton's words, "In the afternoon-evening: realized that the *one thing* that is of any worth whatever in me, the one thing of value, and this is infinitely valuable, is the light to know God, the gift of faith that makes Him present in my heart. He who called forth light from darkness has shone in my heart! (II Cor. 4:6)."

We have the same light, Thomas, and I think we're coming to this point of understanding that if we can properly nurture and, when necessary, nurse our faith, the light will be there in our hearts. And we can always aspire to value it and live it in the world as we are called to do. "Write the light," a friend recently told me.

From time to time, I have experienced the light purely, in a way that summons overflowing gratitude. One spring morning, I was sitting in a drafty barn on the grounds of a local nursery, taking a seminar on how to grow hydrangeas. The day was rainy and chilly, but I was glad that I'd been able to make the time on a Saturday morning to take the class. Instead of cold, I felt extraordinarily warm and happy. A cat named Coleus claimed my lap and sat there purring and snoozing for over an hour—animals don't usually seek me out like this I asked the guy giving the lecture a question about shady conditions, and he told me how I might get an oak leaf hydrangea to survive in my back flower bed. For some reason, I felt so grateful that I wanted to hug him. I was in this ongoing state of joy and awe, of being in love and in wonder. It felt like a Fourth-and-Walnut moment, Thomas, because everyone around me seemed like they were shining like the sun. I saw light everywhere—streaming, glowing everywhere. And I did have the feeling, rich and palpable, that I was loved and I was doing all right.

6

The Soul Selects Its Society

HOW TO MAKE SPIRITUAL FRIENDS

*Although I have always put on a show of being very
ascetic, I do not hesitate to confess that letters from
my friends have always and will always mean a great
deal to me.*

IN AUGUST 1941, THOMAS MERTON, STILL NEW TO HIS
faith and seeking to understand his life's vocation, spent about
three weeks volunteering at Friendship House, a nonprofit
charity in Harlem. He'd met the founder of the organization,
Catherine de Hueck, when she spoke at St. Bonaventure's College in Upstate New York, where Merton was teaching English.
During his time at Friendship House, he led prayer services,
sorted through donated clothing, and looked after children.
The work and the people he met impressed him deeply, and
he felt as though the group "had banded themselves together
to form a small, secret colony of the Kingdom of Heaven in this
earth of exile."

When he left, Merton recognized a void inside him, one
that made him feel thrown back into the world, unanchored

and alone. Being an orphan, this wasn't the first time he had felt alone. But in this instance for Merton, the sensation inspired a poignant realization. "I needed this support, this nearness of those who really loved Christ so much that they seemed to see Him," he writes. "I needed to be with people whose every action told me something of the country that was my home: just as expatriates in every alien land keep together, if only to remind themselves, by their very faces and clothes and gait and accents and expressions, of the land they come from."

✓ The young Merton had hit upon an important requirement for the spiritual journey: companionship. He wasn't the first to understand this necessity. The Irish poet and philosopher John O'Donohue, in his 1997 book *Anam Cara*, writes, "In the early Celtic church, a person who acted as a teacher, companion, or spiritual guide was called an *anam cara*. It originally referred to someone to whom you confessed, revealing the hidden intimacies of your life. With the *anam cara* you could share your inner-most self, your mind and your heart. This friendship was an act of recognition and belonging. When you had an *anam cara*, your friendship cut across all convention, morality, and category. You were joined in an ancient and eternal way with the 'friend of your soul.'"

From his description, it's clear that Merton knew the support he needed wouldn't necessarily be found among all of his friends—and he would come to have a lot of them. Merton, in fact, had a talent for friendship. Over the years, he maintained a vivid correspondence with his Columbia classmates and then, once *The Seven Storey Mountain* was published, a mind-boggling array of artists, writers, students, priests, nuns, and activists. The bulk of these letters were published and take up five volumes. At some point, Merton had realized writing letters from the monastery provided him an opportunity to reach the outside world and develop connections that would have been unavailable to him otherwise. If he came across a book, an article, or a review that he felt was particularly good, he would fire off a letter to the author on his typewriter. He did it like we would dash off a text or an email today. But he also had to find an address for the person and get permission to send a letter when his abbot thought Merton was already too much in touch with the outside world. The abbot probably didn't realize this was like trying to put toothpaste back in the tube.

Sometimes the dialogue that arose from Merton's letters didn't go beyond polite conversation. But sometimes, to his delight, he discovered spiritual compatriots like Boris Pasternak, the Russian author of the novel *Dr. Zhivago*. He first wrote to Pasternak in 1958 and sent him a limited-edition copy of a prose poem Merton had published, *Prometheus: A Meditation*. In one letter, Merton tells him, "With other writers I can share ideas, but you seem to communicate something deeper. It is as if we met on a deeper level of life on which individuals are not separate beings . . . as if we were known to one another in God." Pasternak responds, acknowledging the connection Merton had intuited, and says Merton's letter was "wonderfully filled with kindred thoughts as having been written half by myself."

Later, after receiving a letter from his friend, Merton would write in his journal that Pasternak's correspondence

confirmed my intuition of the deep and fundamental understanding that exists between us. And this is the thing

I have been growing to see is most important: *Everything* hangs on the possibility of such understanding which forms our interior bond that is the only basis of true peace and true community. External juridical, doctrinal etc. bonds can never achieve this. And this bond exists between me and countless people like Pasternak everywhere in the world (genuine people like Pasternak are never "countless") and my vocation is intimately bound up with this bond and this understanding for the sake of which also I have to be solitary and not waste my spirit in pretenses that do not come anywhere near the reality or have anything to do with it.

At the time of their correspondence, Pasternak was enduring immense political pressure from the Soviet government for his work, pressure that intensified when he won the Nobel Prize for Literature and wasn't allowed to accept the award. Merton worried about him and supported him as much as he could. In another entry, Merton writes of his correspondence with Pasternak in a way similar to how he wrote years earlier of his connection with Friendship House: "This simple and human dialogue with Pasternak and a few others like him is to me worth thousands of sermons and radio speeches. It is to me the true King Dom [*sic*] of God, which is still so clearly, and evidently, 'in the midst of us.'"

Such heart-piercing sentences. It's obvious that in special relationships, Merton found hope. The "deep and fundamental understanding" provided affirmation as well as a home for challenging and fruitful dialogue. I have experienced this kind of soulful friendship, and I agree with Merton—connecting with like-spirited people seems to fast-track the journey. O'Donohue writes, "Human presence is a creative and turbulent sacrament, a visible sign of invisible grace. . . . Friendship is the sweet grace that liberates us to approach, recognize, and inhabit this adventure."

In my spiritual friendships, our conversations provide insights I wouldn't have come to on my own. We recognize each other's gifts and encourage each other to use them. I'm more inclined to try something new, to take a risk. On my own, it's like I'm walking the path in semidarkness. I know I'm on it, but since I can't see too far in front of me, I move slowly, cautiously. But the type of friend Merton is talking about can shine light on the path, and I see it so much more clearly. Automatic daylight. Virtual sun. Suddenly I don't have to be slow anymore. I can run.

SOUL CHOICES

How does one find and cultivate such a friendship? We can access so many more people thanks to social media, but somehow an environment known for igniting negativity more than anything else doesn't seem conducive to soul-searing, one-on-one conversations. Besides, it seems this is the kind of search in which one has to feel the way, leading with the heart. Actually, *search* is probably the wrong word. It's been my experience that the friends closest to my heart have shown up when I wasn't looking for them. A friend and I once marveled over how we managed to become friends when, on the surface, we had nothing in common. He shrugged and quoted Emily

Dickinson: "The soul selects her own society." But how in the world does that happen?

When I think of how Merton connected with his soul friends, the key seemed to be showing up somewhere and being totally, unreservedly himself, like laying all of his cards on the table. Of course, I mean "showing up somewhere" figuratively, because he couldn't go anywhere. But the essence is the same, whether he's with a friend in person or via letters: it's about Merton doing his thing. Merton reading widely, Merton praying fervently, Merton shaping with a carpenter's focus and skill his own thinking about the world. Merton not being afraid to communicate this thinking. Merton being so curious and wanting to learn from others. Merton being so joyfully human. When the writer Henri Nouwen first met him, Nouwen was taken aback that Thomas Merton was an "earthy man, dressed in sloppy blue jeans, loud, laughing, friendly and unpretentious." He witnessed Merton being exactly who he was. And because Merton's soul was so completely on display, it was available to attract, like a magnet, the society that would most strengthen it.

Several years ago, when I worked for *People* magazine, I interviewed Sister Helen Prejean, the author of *Dead Man Walking*, about Susan Sarandon, the actress who played her in the film adaptation of the book. She spoke of their first meeting, at a restaurant in New Orleans, and how she was immediately struck by Sarandon. As they sat eating crawfish, Sister Helen had marveled over Sarandon's powerful life force, how she was so interested in everything, and how deeply she seemed to be enjoying her meal. "I was just so attracted to her," Sister Helen said. I told Sister Helen that I really had to ask about her speaking of "attraction"—she was a nun, after all. She explained—and I've never forgotten this—how we're all connected to the earth, and it's like we have magnets within us. We are each attracted to some people and repelled by others. To feel that kind of attraction and energy is rare. When you find a connection with another person, you follow it and honor it.

At the time, I was in my early thirties and suffering from the wrongheaded notion that I could be friends with anyone. I had friends who took energy rather than provided it, to whom I clung in obligation and not love. I didn't realize how much these relationships weighed on me until Sister Helen's words changed my life. She helped me clear out important head and heart space to make room for the meaningful connections that eventually came my way. I've since learned the vital friendships are not always easy—distance and circumstances often make them seem impossible—but I am no longer afraid to pursue them. I follow the energy and I leap into the fire because, as the mystic Rumi says, "If you stay away from the fire, / you will remain sour, doughy, numb, and raw."

THE OBVIOUS PLACE ISN'T ALWAYS THE RIGHT ONE

Can a soul find kinship at church? Surely being in worship with others and sharing the same doctrinal bonds would naturally lead to deep friendships, right? Not necessarily. If it did, then Merton should have been automatically surrounded by spiritual kindred upon entering Gethsemani. Yet as much as he loved his monastery brothers, Merton noted that most of them had no real understanding of him. And sadly, the abbey's very setup meant the brothers remained at a certain distance. The monastery discouraged close connections between the monks and even had regulations against "Particular Friendships."

But Merton did manage to bond with a few. The monk he felt closest to was a young man who went by the name of Father John of the Cross and who became Merton's confessor for a while. Merton knew he was special, noting how attentive all the other monks were whenever it was John of the Cross's turn to preach a sermon. "[He's] one of the few men in this monastery who have anything to say in a sermon," Merton reflects. "What he preaches is really the Gospel." Merton appreciated John's sense of grace, not to mention his willingness to chide Merton, in a way he probably wouldn't have stood for from anyone else, about his ongoing complaints about the monastery: "Fr. John of the Cross said I would have less resentment in me if I were more concentrated on doing whatever it is God wills for me and not considering the defects of this institution."

Unfortunately, John of the Cross had his own troubles at the abbey. "I know the integrity of this man is very costly to him," Merton writes. "He suffers very much in order to be true to his own heart, that is to the heart which God has given him, and which has in it a mysterious command that no one here is able to understand." Merton doesn't give the specifics of the trouble, but his feelings about it are clear:

> What they are continuing to do to Fr. John of the Cross is a shame to mention. Tragic and stupid righteousness with which he is being "brought into line"—made to conform....

But in the end it is the old fear of originality, of the person who has "got something," who realizes that mere conformity would be an infidelity to God and to grace—fear of the man who is different from the others and will not (*can* not) sacrifice that difference which makes them fear him because he is so obviously superior. So he is made to suffer for his superior gifts of heart and mind and soul.

John of the Cross eventually left Gethsemani on what was supposed to be a leave of absence. He never returned.

What strikes me in Merton's writing about his friend is how Merton respected John of the Cross's faith and how John expressed that faith even though Merton probably didn't understand it and no matter what the nonconformity may have been. Merton demonstrated the importance of respecting God's presence in someone no matter how it shows up. This would inform all of Merton's relationships, especially his encounters with Zen and Buddhist teachers during his studies and dialogue on Eastern beliefs.

How you must have missed your friend, Thomas. When I think about your famous epiphany on Fourth and Walnut in Louisville, I wonder if you wanted to run back and share it with someone at the monastery. Would you have been disappointed if you had tried? Sometimes I have this experience at church. I'll read something, or have an insight during a worship service, and try to talk about it either one-on-one with someone or in a group session. It rarely leads to understanding or dialogue.

But one time it did. I had carpooled with a group to hear a spiritual speaker in another town. The talk lit me up, and on the way home, the people in the car with me had a spirited conversation. That conversation expanded on our experience of the talk and how we would use what we had learned. The conversation helped me shape my thoughts for an essay I eventually wrote on the talk and why it had so moved me. A few days later, I was surprised to learn the people in one of the other cars didn't discuss the talk on the drive home—at all. If I had been in that car, I would have been frustrated, sitting and staring out the window and feeling like a flower bud closed tightly because the air was too cold for it to bloom. In discussing this difference with another person who had attended the talk, I came to understand, with compassion, how most people deal with their lives and spirituality: they simply don't engage. They don't attend to the interior life, to the questions and ideas that arise. Maybe the driver and passengers in the other car had been stirred up by the talk as well but were too harried to wrap their brains around it. Perhaps their minds were already on the chores waiting at home, the deadlines waiting at the office. They didn't want to think about the spirituality that might turn their lives upside down. My friend even inferred that this is the way many Episcopalians are—or at least New England ones. I still think about those car rides and about how grateful I am that I landed in one car and not the other. I still think about how much it matters who travels with me.

IN THE OPEN FIELD

When a publisher asked me and writer Susanna Childress to curate an essay series on the topic of religion, I saw it as an opportunity to open windows and bring fresh air to this very closed-up question. People aren't comfortable engaging with religion. We can't discuss it in polite conversation, and if we do, it threatens to become a source of division rather than a source of ideas and renewal. It's as if our society has put religion in a box of restrictions, and these restrictions are limits we've created with small minds and little imagination.

The popular phrase these days (and I think Merton would be intrigued by this) is "I am spiritual but not religious." Author Barbara Brown Taylor, in the introduction to her book *An Altar in the World: A Geography of Faith*, writes that if she had a dol- lar for every time she heard the phrase, "I might not be any wiser about what that means—but I would be richer." Taylor describes how the spiritual-but-not-religious crowd wants to "grow closer to God, but not at the cost of creeds, confessions, and religious wars large or small." They cobble together guiding wisdom from a variety of books and experiences, but, Taylor writes, "plenty of them are satisfied, too, even as they confess that they are sometimes lonely." I'm wondering if, when religion gets put in a box, some aspect of ourselves gets boxed up as well. I wonder if the spiritual but not religious people take themselves out of a realm where they could make the kind of vital friendship Merton describes.

One of my favorite pieces of Scripture is Isaiah 55:8–9: "For my thoughts are not your thoughts, nor are your ways my ways, says the Lord. For as the heavens are higher than the earth, so are my ways higher than your ways, and my thoughts than your thoughts." These words tell me the way of the spirit is expansive—hugely so. And we are meant to be just as expansive when we seek God in whatever form. I believe there are these glowing areas where religion and spirituality can go hand in hand, one feeding the other. I have encountered a variety of writers, all pursuing spirituality in various faiths. They have a fullness of expression touching on the ritual, the spiritual, and the visceral, showing what faith can look like as it shows up in everyday life.

The poet and mystic Rumi wrote, "Out beyond ideas of right and wrongdoing, there is a field. I will meet you there." I feel like I'm standing with these writers, and with Merton too, in this open field. We are reaching for our higher thoughts, seeking a place of engagement and not a limitation or close-mindedness.

 I recognize this seeking in Merton's interactions with teachers, especially those of Eastern philosophies. Merton first wrote to Dr. Daisetz T. Suzuki, a noted Zen master, in March 1959. Suzuki's teachings often explored the bridging of Buddhist and Christian mysticism, and Merton had read most of his books. He opened a dialogue by showing Suzuki he was willing to learn: "I will not be so foolish as to pretend to you that I understand Zen. To be frank, I hardly understand Christianity." There's nothing deep about this first communication. In fact, besides praising Suzuki, the letter asks him to write an introduction for a book Merton was working on, a translation of the sayings of the Egyptian desert monks of the fourth and fifth centuries.

However, in Merton's journals, he shows that his interest in Suzuki was for the long term, and he was already doing some careful thinking about how their dialogue and relationship would progress. He understood that such interaction would turn on trusting in God as well as each man expressing respect for who the other was and what he believed:

> If I should demand that Suzuki should come over and meet me on this ground that is alien to us both: it would be a terrible infidelity to Truth, to myself, and to Christ. . . . Thus if I tried baldly and bluntly to "convert" Suzuki, that is, make him "accept" formulas regarding the faith that are accepted by the average American Catholic, I would, in fact, not "convert" him at all, but simply confuse and (in a cultural sense) degrade him. . . . If I can meet him on common ground of spiritual Truth, where we share a real and deep experience of God, and where we know in humility our own deepest selves—and if we can discuss and compare the formulas we use to describe this experience, then I certainly think Christ would be present and glorified in both of us and this would lead to a *conversion of us both*—an elevation, a development, a serious growth in Christ.

Suzuki appreciated Merton's eagerness and candor. They shared writing and books and learned from each other despite Suzuki's being much older than Merton. In fact, the only reason they were finally able to meet in person in New York City in 1964 was because Merton had pleaded the case to his abbot that Suzuki's age, ninety-four, and frail health meant they would be unlikely to have another chance to see each other.

At the joyful meeting, the two men drank tea and enjoyed talking despite Merton having to yell in Suzuki's ear to be heard. At the end of their sessions, Suzuki left Merton with one simple message. He said, "The most important thing is Love."

There's a perfection I like about the image of the Eastern teacher and the Western monk meeting on common ground and sharing experiences of God. Most certainly, God was present and glorified. It was the essence of Rumi's open field.

A MIRROR OF GENEROSITY

The concept of spiritual friendship can feel like fog in the hands—hard to grasp, hard to seek. Maybe the difficulty helps us remember that God is at work here as well. There's something of the divine in how a friend shows up. In *Conjectures of a Guilty Bystander*, Merton quotes his friend Jacques Maritain, the French Catholic philosopher, who acknowledges that special connections are truly a blessing: "One is paid for one's trouble by that which is best in the world, that marvel of those friendships which God awakens and of the pure fidelities which He inspires and which are like a mirror of the gratuity and generosity of His love."

Maritain's words fit the sense I have of friends being an abundance of God's love flowing over us when we most need it. Whenever I have been most in despair, God has responded with a person. One evening last year when I was driving to the meeting of a prayer group, I had a moment in the car when I thought to myself, "This is what despair feels like." I felt angry and overwhelmed, and though in such moments it's supposed to help to be grateful for things, I could only think of what I didn't have. It was the kind of dark thinking I would have if I had not slept, like when my son was a baby or if I had pulled an all-nighter. But this was bigger, as though I had been doing an all-nighter for eight weeks in a row.

It was summer, but I hadn't yet had any kind of break, and no break was in sight—no time to myself at all. Since the school year ended, I had been volunteering for my son's summer theater group, finding housing for the out-of-town staff. I was teaching a class in an MFA program, doing homework for the course I was taking to earn a graduate certificate in online teaching, and preparing and teaching classes and workshops in New Jersey. My family had recently returned from Ohio, where I had attended both a family reunion and my high school reunion. When we returned home, I still had papers to grade and homework to do and no time to write. And no time to rest. I had a note in my calendar to start work on my application for a fellowship, but just looking at the foundation's website made me feel I hadn't done enough in my writing career, certainly nothing like the fellows named last year had accomplished. I was thinking, *When am I supposed to do more? When can I get serious work done while still running this family and making money?* I had to keep making money. That month we'd taken a huge financial hit: We had to replace both the water heater and the furnace in our home. The brakes on my van needed replacing. The mortgage had to be paid. I'd heard nothing from my agent on the book proposals she'd submitted, so there was no book advance anywhere on the horizon.

So driving to the prayer group that evening, I was in this frustrated spiral, feeling worse and worse about my lack of time and resources. I was thinking about how I probably wouldn't have the kind of deep, clarifying, spiritual conversation I obviously needed to have. Suddenly I pulled into the parking lot of a store, thinking maybe I should just buy a lottery ticket. I figured what I really needed was a big chunk of money and some hope. But I soon realized this was ridiculous thinking, which showed how far down a rabbit hole I'd fallen. I shifted the van back into drive and continued to my church.

When I got there, I sat in the parking lot for a few minutes listening to a song on the radio, hoping that would help me feel better. Then, opposite me in the lot, I saw my friend Rick get out of his car. I hadn't seen him in months because he had switched to a church in an urban location. I'd sorely missed our conversations about faith and imagination, about different ways to pray. He had been one of the few people with whom I could share my spiritual adventures. Rick modeled for me patience, compassion, and cheerfulness. I found his faith, which led him to work tirelessly for social justice, so inspiring. In fact, he was in the parking lot because he'd come to meet with an interfaith group that helps refugee families moving to the United States. Their meeting would be across the hall from my prayer group.

I practically flew from my van and went to hug him. He told me he knew what I was up to because he follows me on Facebook, and he said how much he appreciates my posts. "You put something of your soul in them," he said. I was grateful for this, because in that moment, I probably needed affirmation of any kind. I told him how glad I was to know he's still doing his good work, but of course I never doubted that. I felt an enormous charge of energy. The evening light glowed. Everything looked so different.

I'm very aware that if I had gone in the store to buy that lottery ticket, I would have missed seeing Rick in the parking lot. When I sat down for the prayer group, I found it hard to focus and listen because I was buzzing, like I was already talking to God. I wanted to go outside and walk the labyrinth in the churchyard and contemplate what had just happened. I was feeling weak and humbled because the gift of that brief encounter with Rick made me realize how deep my anger and despair had been. I was lost and adrift in an unknown land. I needed someone, as the young Merton had, to tell me "something of the country that was my home." God, simply and sublimely, brought such a person to me. I know for certain that one way or another, this will always be the case—the friends will be there when I need them most.

7

Human in an Inhuman Age
HOW TO SERVE THE WORLD

*Ever since my baptism I have been of small faith, weak
and insecure and impatient and without strength or
courage.*

MY HUSBAND GETS IMPATIENT ABOUT WHAT I DON'T
know about current events. He doesn't understand. For fifteen
years, as a magazine journalist, I was steeped in the news. I
scanned four to six newspapers daily: the *New York Times*, the
Washington Post, the *New York Post*, the *New York Daily News*,
the *Wall Street Journal*, and *USA Today*. Add to that the Associated Press newswire and the filed reports from our publication's bureau correspondents for whatever story I was working
on that week. I lived with National Public Radio in my ears.

I remember the horror of the genocide in Rwanda, paging
through the photos of bodies piled upon bodies as I prepared
to write a brief piece for *Time* magazine's coverage of the
atrocity. I remember the shock of energy running through my
veins after my husband woke me from a nap on our vacation
to tell me Princess Diana had died and how I ran through the

house to find a phone so I could call my editor. Then 9/11, sitting in a story meeting with everyone stunned to the core, the Twin Towers burning on television screens in every office. They would collapse not long after.

It has taken me this long—almost another fifteen years of not working as a journalist—to wring myself out.

A change in world events, though, required my return to watching the news. I had to be informed about the COVID-19 virus that was making its way through the world like an insidious fog. I had to stay on top of the details because they changed constantly, sometimes within a day. I watched multiple newscasts to learn what time I could go to the grocery store, when it became mandatory to wear a face mask, how long my son would be out of school, what progress had been made toward a vaccine.

This meant my eyes were on the screen when police announced the search for Peter Manfredonia, a University of Connecticut senior who had grown up in our town of Sandy Hook. Manfredonia was now on the run after allegedly killing two people, including a childhood friend of his who lived only ten miles from my house. Even as they tracked him south, I made sure our doors were locked and kept an eye out for strangers walking down our street.

In watching the news, I became an unwilling witness to the video of a Minneapolis police officer calmly kneeling on the neck of George Floyd, an unarmed Black man, until he passed out and died.

When authorities announced Manfredonia's capture, not long after Floyd's death, I stared at the screen, reeling. An armed, 6'4" twentysomething white former football player who had killed two people, kidnapped another, and led authorities on a multistate manhunt had been apprehended safely and quietly, while an unarmed Black man was apprehended by police and was dead. I felt like I couldn't swallow. I had . . . no . . . words.

The travesties of the world used to make me want to cloister myself, shaking my head as I went. Strangely enough, the coronavirus pandemic caused me—and millions of others—to check out from society. We were under stay-at-home orders for weeks. "We're all monks now," Dr. Gregory Hillis noted in an article for *America* magazine. After what I saw on the news—Minneapolis and other cities burning for days and a president who could only say the situation was "not good"—I was inclined to stay cloistered. I was stunned that civility and kindness are mere bubbles that appear and float around to others in times of trial but pop quickly because, as a society, we seem to preserve them only for those we like: people who think like we do and who look like we do. We push the value of life to the outer margins and remain in deep denial until our separation explodes into senseless tragedy and we fall into cold, dark depths. I looked at images of Manfredonia walking on railroad tracks and toting a duffel bag of firearms. We neither keep guns away from those who would do harm nor do enough to give needed help to those who do the harming.

My son, Tain, was a third-grader at Sandy Hook Elementary School in Newtown, Connecticut, that day in December 2012 when a twenty-year-old walked into the school and killed twenty children and six adults. Ben, one of Tain's closest friends and the son of Tain's godmother, was among the deceased. In the wake of such grief, life is distilled to basic moments. I remember holding Tain as he cried at Ben's funeral. I took walks with Ben's mom. I watched Tain from our windows when he went out in our yard that winter, because at school he couldn't go out for recess, but he was ready to play outside again. (Tain and I tell the story of our family's faith practice and how it sustained us after the tragedy in the book we wrote together, *This Child of Faith: Raising a Spiritual Child in a Secular World.*)

I didn't take an active stance on gun control, mainly because right after the tragedy I was focused on simply getting by, day to day. In recent years, I just felt bewildered and hopeless about the issue. Ever since my son came home after the shooting, my calling has been to walk a very particular road with him, through grief and recovery and our family's spiritual growth. I've seen politicians stare into the faces of parents who have lost children and hold that gaze of carefully practiced frozen compassion. They know in their hearts what is right but remain steadfastly ruled by their brains, which tell them how invested they are elsewhere.

I'm not sure what I would say to such a person.

THE EFFECTS OF SOLITUDE

I'm not sure what I would be doing if I didn't have a son for whom I must model a way of being in the world. But sometimes a hermitage seems like a really good place to be. From what I've seen of quarantine on my social media, sheltering in place comes a close second. Pictures of homemade iced cinnamon rolls and crusty brown loaves of bread, pencil drawings of a koala bear, watercolors of flowers, people singing and dancing, one of my college classmates doing yoga on live video once a week: it seemed like we all turned within and found something of the best of ourselves.

Yet a hermitage is not where I'm supposed to be. Somehow I sense this. I'm supposed to be saying something, doing something. And yet I feel anything I could offer would get swallowed up in the noise—I'd be an infant crying out into a hurricane. I stand on the edge of an abyss, my hands in my pockets, and I consider the leap. I feel as though Thomas stands next to me in a similar stance. He helps me think about the possibilities. I think he'd say I have to get out there. I have to find a way to serve. He'd definitely say my hermitage idea is wrongheaded.

"The contemplative life is not, and cannot be, a mere withdrawal, a pure negation, a turning of one's back on the world with its sufferings, its crises, its confusions and its errors," he writes. "The attempt would be illusory. No man can withdraw completely from the society of his fellow men." When he entered the monastery after months of spiritual struggle, Merton described a lightness, as of a door closing or a leaving of the world. He was caught up, as most young men are, with his own journey and the still-bright fascination of his conversion. His writings from his earlier years focused mainly on the cultivation of interior spirituality: *The Seven Storey Mountain*, *Seeds of Contemplation*, *The Ascent to Truth*, *Thoughts in Solitude*, and *The Sign of Jonas*. But as he matured, both emotionally and spiritually, he too sensed there was more—way more—he could be doing. The world, the very state of it, required that he bring his voice to the table.

By the end of the 1950s, the threat of nuclear war loomed over the country. Merton felt impelled to speak out, but his ✓ position as a monk dedicated by vow to silence and solitude held him back. Also, no priest or bishop in the Catholic Church had spoken on peace—he knew he would face opposition because, due to his influence, whatever he wrote, it would seem as though he were speaking for the church. He decided to press forward anyway. In 1961, he wrote his first article on *Agree?* ✓ peace, "The Root of War Is Fear," and laid out the place for Christians in the struggle for peace. He writes, "The duty of the Christian in this crisis is to strive with all his power and intelligence, with his faith, hope in Christ, and love for God and man, to do the one task which God has imposed upon us in the world today. That task is to work for the total abolition of war."

Merton struggled with censors over the new material, and his readers weren't happy with his change in subject matter, but he saw it as the inevitable next phase of his spiritual growth. In the introduction to Merton's book *Passion for Peace*, X author William H. Shannon writes, "What had happened to him was that his solitude had issued into what all true solitude must eventually become: compassion. This sense of compassion moved him to look once again at the world he thought he had left irrevocably twenty years earlier, in 1941, when he had entered the monastery. He now felt a duty, *precisely because he was a contemplative*, to speak out."

As I think about my path to speaking out, the Merton I walk with is sometimes the mature writer of peace and nonviolent protest. But other times it is a young Tom, not yet a monk, walking through New York City in 1939, attending the World's

Fair in Queens and the Picasso exhibition at the Museum of Modern Art. I think of the younger Merton because I feel the activism of the mature Merton began with his observances of the 1939 version of himself. He had the impatience of youth and a frustration with how things in the world were not what they ought to have been. He had no sympathy for how people were behaving:

> But the El Grecos were hung in a small room where you could not see them properly because, if you got more than three feet away from them, people crowded in front of you, peering at the name of the painter, or the little plaque on the bottom of the frame, and then rushing on.
>
> It would be utterly commonplace to say almost all the people going through the exhibit rushed from room to room reading the names of painters off the frames, and not looking at the pictures at all. That is getting to be a very corny joke: the *Punch* jokes about American tourists in the '90s, and so on.

At the Picasso exhibit, which he visited more than once, he noted that most viewers hated Picasso's work and weren't afraid to say it. "These expressions of hatred were excited, almost hysterical; they were shameful and transformed the people who uttered the opinions into beasts," young Thomas writes. "[Two men] ran from picture to picture, obviously whipped white inside; their lips trembled with fear; they tittered like high school girls. One of them would stick his nose an inch from the picture and cry 'Look, Look, he put one coat on top of another too fast, and now the paint's cracked' and he would giggle nervously and rush on to the next one, where, if the paint happened to be cracked, he would say exactly the same thing."

"Ridiculous," I would have said to Thomas if we had been walking together and he had shared that story. I could have offered another example in return—of people who, over-whelmed by the enormity of a truth before them, can only comfort themselves by denying it. What would he have said if I told him about the people who say Sandy Hook never hap-pened? Or the ones who believe the COVID-19 pandemic was all a hoax? Or those who thought the protests in the wake of George Floyd's death were an overreaction?

Then perhaps we would have discussed something like grace, and perhaps Thomas would have guided me to the uncomfortable notion that we are in the same position as these discomfited people. Faced with the enormity of the world's confusion, we see ourselves as mute and lacking. In the month after his journal entries about the Picasso exhibit, Thomas writes of the world tiptoeing on the edge of World War II. Yes, he putters around with reading and poetry and movies, but he's also wrestling with spiritual doubt. "Ever since my baptism I have been of small faith, weak and inse-cure and impatient and without strength or courage," he writes.

Is this what I am? I know the way I'm seeing things is very small and stingy. And perhaps something about my faith gives me these tendencies. I am judgmental. Because I have a vision of the peaceable kingdom in my eyes, I measure the world by this and see it lacking. Because I have in my eyes the bounty of God's table, I am ever more aware of the world starving.

But why is my instinct to retreat instead of doing something about it? How do I reconcile the broad expanse of this abyss? Thomas says a writer's attitude toward life is important. This may be my issue. On the surface, I can muster feelings of cheerfulness for a while, but the edge of stinginess and judgment cuts through me. How do I rub away this dinginess so that love shines through, lighting my way first to a brighter place and not to judgment?

A CHILD'S HEART BETRAYED

There's a short story by Anton Chekhov, "A Trifle from Real Life," in which a child confides to his mother's lover that the nanny takes him to visit his papa. The man promises not to reveal the child's secret to the boy's mother, but for his own selfish purposes, he does. It ends with this sentence about the boy: "This was the first time in his life that he had come roughly face to face with deceit; he had never imagined until now that there were things in this world besides pasties and watches and sweet pears, things for which no name could be found in the vocabulary of childhood."

I am like that child, wild-eyed and indignant in my sense of betrayal. It is my childlike heart that is breaking. And it breaks over disappointments large and small: from realizing that winners of reality show contests are decided more by the producers of the show than by talent to witnessing a video in which a police officer shoots an unarmed Black man dead and then acts as if it's no different from hitting a bird with a BB gun. Add to all this a president who can behave like a petulant child, insensitive to the gravity of the ramifications of his behavior. Who could have thought such behavior could be found in the world?

But these things speak to one truth: The world is one way, and I want it to be another way. And if I hold to that desire, I would be consenting to daily, even hourly, heartbreak. When I was in high school, my favorite radio station played classic hits, and I remember being fascinated by the lyrics of Simon and Garfunkel's "I Am a Rock": "A rock feels no pain and an island never cries." Enticing, I thought, and I even voiced this to a girl sitting next to me in my math class as a possible way of being. She told me, essentially, that I wasn't meant to live like that. A teenager as wise as Merton, who already knew no one is an island? Perhaps.

THE VOICE OF FAITH AND SOCIAL JUSTICE

Merton biographer Michael Mott notes that by the spring of 1962, "Merton's public image had been radically changed. Many a Catholic father who had given *The Seven Storey Mountain* to a restless son must have been baffled, as, perhaps, the son was also." The monk who had taught them quiet spirituality was suddenly being very loud about nuclear warfare and about Vietnam. But in many venues, Merton's outspoken views were met with acceptance and appreciation. During Holy Week in April, his "Prayer for Peace" was read in the US House of Representatives and included the following admonition: "Let us never forget that sins against the law of love are punishable by loss of faith, and those without faith stop at no crime to achieve their ends! Help us to be masters of the weapons that threaten to master us. Help us to use our science for peace and plenty, not for war and destruction." A few weeks later, the head of Merton's order forbade him to write about peace. He also vetoed publication of a book Merton had just finished, *Peace in the Post-Christian Era.* "The decision seems to be that I am to stop all publication of anything on war," Merton writes in his journal. "In other words I am to be in effect silenced on this subject for the main reason that it is not appropriate for a monk, and that it 'falsifies the message of monasticism.'"

I have no idea what "the message of monasticism" is supposed to be. It sounds like Merton was supposed to demonstrate how to stay cloistered, pray, and say nothing. I don't understand the tensions that still exist in many faith communities between engaging with issues such as peace and racial injustice and staying out of it all. So much of Christian teaching is about addressing wrongs. Ephesians 6:14–17 even provides instructions for how to suit up for a fight: "Stand therefore, and fasten the belt of truth around your waist, and put on the breastplate of righteousness. As shoes for your feet put on whatever will make you ready to proclaim the gospel of peace. With all of these, take the shield of faith, with which you will be able to quench all the flaming arrows of the evil one. Take the helmet of salvation, and the sword of the Spirit, which is the word of God."

I used to think when I joined a faith community that it would be a place where we talked about the world's wrongs in addition to worshipping God. I learned, however, during a casual conversation with the rector of our church that she, and in fact most ministers leading congregations, has to be very careful about how often to bring up social issues in a sermon. Most people want their faith and worship neat and uncluttered by challenging or divisive ideas. I was flummoxed.

At first I thought what she told me must be a characteristic of mostly white New England churches. Then, at a spiritual writers' conference, I met Frank A. Thomas, who teaches homiletics and African American preaching at Christian Theological Seminary in Indianapolis. He confirmed what my rector had said. He'd even written a book, *How to Preach a Dangerous Sermon*, and said in it that every time he steps into a pulpit, he has to make a decision: "If I participate in preaching smooth patriotism and evangelism divorced from the lack of material prospects of the marginalized, or preach an over-promised gospel of wealth and prosperity that benefits the few instead of a dangerous gospel to serve the poor, then when I lay my head on the pillow at night, I am a non-Christian and nonperson. I must call myself to conscience."

Frank Thomas defines a dangerous sermon as one that "challenges unjust moral orders and dominance hierarchies and the resulting misallocation of freedom, resources, assets, and legitimacy. [It] disrupts the legitimacy of the oppressive moral order." And by moral, he's talking about issues such as health care and the fact that a person can lose his or her life savings from one medical emergency. That's just plain wrong, so it's a moral issue. He also admitted the dire backlash some ministers face for preaching challenging material. He even wrote a sequel, *Surviving a Dangerous Sermon*, to answer questions he'd received from pastors about how to preach this way and stay employed. Because people leave churches and want heads to roll when they are challenged. They fire the ministers who do the challenging. I realize some people only want their faith on their terms. Merton writes often of the desire to please God, and I sometimes wonder where that desire in our society has gone.

THE LOOK OF PROTEST

The public face of protest can be daunting. As I write, Minneapolis is burning over the death of an unarmed Black man in police custody. Protesters are facing down officers who are wearing riot gear and tossing tear gas to disperse the crowd. I think about the people who must be burning on the inside, parsing for themselves whether to be out in the streets with their outrage or to seethe on their own at home. Merton himself had a mistrust of and distaste for large-scale demonstrations. "We tend to think massive protest is all that is valid today," he writes. "But the massive is also manipulated and doctored. It is false. The genuine dissent remains individual. At least that is my option. In my view it is saner and nobler to take the kind of view E. M. Forster takes, not line up with the manipulated group. But to the group this looks like defeat. It looks like futility."

In 1965, as America's engagement with the Vietnam War intensified, the protests followed suit. At the time, Merton had been aligned with a group called the Catholic Peace Fellowship (CPF), an organization started the previous year with the aim of counseling conscientious objectors. But the group's protest activities, including burning draft cards, went far beyond the comfort level for Merton, who favored the methods of nonviolence taught by Gandhi and used notably by Martin Luther King Jr. in the civil rights movement. When a young man connected to the group set fire to himself in front of the United Nations Building in New York City, Merton had had enough. He wired a telegram requesting his name be removed from the CPF's list of sponsors. He worried his reaction had been too harsh: "But with things as crazy as they are I cannot let my name be used by an outfit as unpredictable as that is, with kids likely to do anything at any moment. . . . The world has never been so sick. Demonstrations. Counterdemonstrations. And all of it in the realm of signs and gestures, agitation—meaning what? The war in Viet Nam goes on and the only effect of the demonstrations is that the general run of people get scared and accept the war because at least it is familiar!"

There seems to be all-or-nothing thinking in our society when it comes to demonstrations. You're either out in the streets or you're sitting on your hands at home. But I'm learning there are many people, especially millennials, who are looking for their own authentic way to dissent. They don't want to be tagged as "slacktivists." Slacktivism describes "the minimal efforts people engage in, often by means of social media, to 'support' an issue or cause, but that have minimal or no practical effect. These produce mostly a sense of self-satisfaction from having done 'something good.'" Yet they want to make a difference.

I believe I stand in the place of individual dissent Merton described. I look for opportunities where I can be most effective, doing something specific that only I or few others can do. Usually this means writing. But when the Sandy Hook tragedy occurred, I was a licensed school bus driver. I've never been comfortable participating in large demonstrations, but when the first organized protests against gun violence were scheduled to take place in the state capital, I saw something specific I could do, so I drove one of the buses transporting people from my community to the event. I felt I'd made a contribution—and an effective one. I'm sure there are those who would disagree.

But Thomas is telling me it's OK. I don't have to be perfect, saintly, pure of heart. He certainly wasn't, and he even figured that was why his readers liked him: "It seems to me that one of the reasons why my writing appeals to many people is precisely that I am not so sure of myself and do not claim to have all the answers." So I only have to step forward in my own vulnerable, broken, unkind, silly humanity. And I need to keep writing. I feel, as Thomas once did, I've come to a starting point: "The conviction that I have not yet even begun to write, to think, to pray, and to live and that only now I am getting down to waking up." So I have to seek each and every opportunity to build on my work. Create something more despite not knowing what "more" might look like. Pray to be OK in this place of not knowing.

CALLINGS

Recently I was in Indianapolis teaching at a spiritual writers' conference. After one of my classes, a woman came up to me and told me she owns an independent bookstore, but she's also a lawyer and has been doing work on gun control laws. She asked me about the issue, and I wasn't sure how to communicate the depth of my disillusionment. Gun control is actually a dozen issues, maybe more, concerning personal freedoms, the Second Amendment of the US Constitution, corporate power, mental health, privacy, and political influence. Each aspect of these issues pushes up against another. Nothing moves forward. The enormity of the mess just stupefies me. I responded to the woman only briefly. I told her that since nothing had changed after all the lives that had been lost, I doubted anything would really change now.

Less than two hours later came the news that the Connecticut Supreme Court would allow to move forward a lawsuit, brought by a group of Sandy Hook families, against a gun manufacturer. I was happily stunned to be proven wrong—and so quickly. I sought out the woman and, with tears in my eyes, told her the news. We rejoiced together, and then she said something to me that I will never forget.

"It's all right. We are here to do this work for you," she said gently. "You lived through it, and that's enough."

This is my calling, she was saying. I realized when I had responded to her earlier that I was speaking from a place of darkness and no hope. She handed hope back to me, a butterfly with gentle, golden wings.

The following week, just six days after the massacre in the Christchurch mosque, New Zealand's government passed legislation banning a range of semiautomatic rifles and large-ammunition magazines. The day after that, the state senate in Vermont passed a bill requiring a waiting period to purchase a handgun. Hope began to glow.

I carried this hope to St. James's Episcopal Church in West Hartford, Connecticut, where I had been invited to speak for their Lenten series "Walking the Talk: Living Our Baptismal Promises." The baptismal vow I spoke to was "Will you persevere in resisting evil and, whenever you fall into sin, repent and return to the Lord?" I talked about my recent experiences and how we don't resist alone. Sometimes the work is yours, and sometimes it belongs to others. And it's OK.

In the Old Testament, God, having observed the misery of the people, calls out to Moses with vital work to do: "So come, I will send you to Pharaoh to bring my people, the Israelites, out of Egypt" (Exod 3:10). I've come to understand that a calling is a complex thing. My struggles are warranted, because usually the work of a calling is hard and not necessarily something anyone wants to do. You doubt your abilities; you doubt the outcome. You grapple to feel the support of faith, of understanding God's "I will be with you."

But my encounter with the woman at the conference had clarified for me a much-needed piece for discernment I had only guessed at before: Sometimes you answer a call because there is work to be done that others cannot do. Moses answered a call because there were others who could watch after the flock, but not everyone could lead the Israelites out of Egypt. I pray I will recognize new callings when they emerge for me. I hope I'll be able to step into a void and serve where someone else feels hopeless, just as the woman had done for me.

8

The Hermione Granger of Gethsemani

HOW TO PRAY

I am not going to write as one driven by compulsions—but freely, because I am a writer, and because for me to write is to think and to live and also in some degree even to pray.

THOMAS MERTON WANTED TO BE ALONE. TO BE MORE specific, he wanted a place to be alone. When he entered the Abbey of Gethsemani, he had assumed he would have a serene existence. Before becoming a monk, he had once gone on retreat at the monastery, and he had enjoyed the hours he'd spent in silence, praying, reading, and reflecting. And despite living the boisterous life of a twentysomething guy, he'd always had time to sit and think and quiet spaces of his own in which to do so—his one-room apartment on Perry Street in New York's Greenwich Village, and his room at St. Bonaventure's College where he taught English.

But Merton quickly learned that the experience of a monk was different from that of a retreat guest and was full of busyness and distraction. The abbey schedule during the 1940s was highly structured and relentless, including study and physical labor on the monastery's farm. And as for prayer, their main activity, the monks prayed together around the clock, starting with rising at 2:00 a.m. for Matins and Lauds of Our Lady's Office and continuing with Meditation at 2:30 a.m., the Night Office at 3 a.m., and then priests saying private masses at 4:00 a.m., followed by reading or private prayer. Prime was at 5:30 a.m.; then Tierce, High Mass, and Sext took place, one after the other, starting at 7:45 a.m. None was at 11:07 a.m. and Vespers at 4:30 p.m., and then they ended the day with Compline at 6:10 p.m. Bedtime was at 7:00 p.m. in the winter and 8:00 p.m. in the summer. Merton would finish his days exhausted, although he should have had plenty of time for solitude and reflection. At least five spaces on the schedule allowed for reading and "private prayer."

But Gethsemani was growing, getting ever more crowded. The monastery had been built to house between fifty and seventy monks, but with an influx of ex-soldiers after the close of World War II, by 1946 the number in residence was nearing two hundred. And that was before publication of *The Seven Storey Mountain*, which increased Gethsemani's popularity. Merton had trouble sleeping in the dormitory and also felt he needed a place just to recharge and settle after the energy required to be in a large group. In today's terms, he probably would have been labeled as the kind of introvert who can enjoy being around people but requires time to recover from the encounters. So Merton sought out small, secluded spaces on the monastery's property—one was a tool shed, another the attic of a garden house that had a window from which he could view the valley. At one point he even sat in a derelict trailer in the woods.

Merton's particular order, the Cistercians, didn't have solitude as part of their "rule of life," which are the guidelines that describe how a faith community shapes its way of living. His superiors, though giving him time and space for his writing, refused to entertain Merton's repeated suggestions that he become a hermit and somehow live apart from the monastery.

"The answer, his superiors and spiritual advisers told him over and over, was *inner* solitude, detachment, a hermitage of the heart: he needed no physical place of solitude," writes his biographer, Michael Mott. They did make a concession by permitting him, in the summer of 1949, to walk alone in the woods outside the monastery's enclosure.

Merton still cultivated other ideas. He thought about switching to a more contemplative monastic order, such as the Carthusians or the Camaldolese, which allowed monks to have their own separate hermitages. In the late 1950s, Merton solicited outright to move to a monastery in Mexico—a request that was denied in 1959.

However, Merton chipped away at the monastery's resistance and finally had his prayer for private space answered, in part, when in 1961 Gethsemani's abbot allowed for the building of a small structure that would eventually become Merton's hermitage. I say "in part" because initially Merton was allowed to visit the building only at certain times of the day. It was months before he was given permission to sleep there and not until August 1965 that he was allowed to live there full time. The concrete-block structure with its small porch stood less than a mile from the monastery, within earshot of the church bells. There were tall pines in the wooded area behind it and a lawn and a view of the valley in front. The living space was quite basic, with a fireplace but no electricity or running water, just an outhouse.

Merton loved it: "Everything about this hermitage simply fills me with joy. There are lots of things that could have been far more perfect one way or another—ascetically, or 'domestically.' But it is the place God has given me after so much prayer and longing—and without my deserving it—and it is a delight."

The first night he slept in the hermitage, which he called St. Mary of Carmel, was after a large conference hosted at the monastery. He writes, "It finally helped me to get the noise and agitation of the Abbots' meeting out of my system. . . . A deep sense of peace and truth. That this was the way things are supposed to be, that I was in my right mind for a change." And the following morning, he reports, "[I] lit the fire and said Lauds quietly, slowly, thoughtfully, sitting on the floor. I felt very much alive, and real, and awake, surrounded by silence and penetrated by truth. Wonderful smell of pre-dawn woods and fields in the cold night!"

Initially, when reading Merton's multitude of journal entries about his desire for solitude, I did get a little impatient. I didn't understand his need, nor why he couldn't settle for concessions that no other monks had ever been allowed. But then I thought about how solitude feels for me, especially if I'm out walking prayerfully in the early morning and can sense the exquisite ache of a connection to God. I realized Merton's request, ultimately, wasn't about solitude. It was about prayer. He probably did need time by himself to recharge after teaching and preaching and speaking in abbey meetings. But I think what he found in sitting by himself was another level of prayer.

He noticed it during his writing sessions: "At the moment the writing is the one thing that gives me access to some real silence and solitude. Also I find that it helps me to pray because, when I pause at my work, I find that the mirror inside me is surprisingly clean and deep and serene and God shines there and is immediately found, without hunting, as if He had come close to me while I was writing and I had not observed His coming. And this I think should be the cause of great joy, and to me it is."

Merton had managed a deep connection with Spirit and desired to attain it again and again. In *Thomas Merton's Gethsemani*, writer Monica Weis comments on the trailer in the woods Merton once used for prayer, saying, "In this rusted metal chapel, which he regarded as an entrance to paradise, Merton heard the Holy One calling him 'friend' and 'son.' He felt the sleeping seed of prayer awaken.... Yet he continued to hunger for more frequent and more sustained opportunities for communion with the divine."

If that's what Merton heard and felt, then I don't blame him. That sense of the Lord drawing near is really *everything*. I'd be knocking on the abbot's office door daily to state my case if that's what I needed to do in order to have that feeling of Spirit again. I think there's such a thing as spiritual noise—it's hard to hear God when everyone in the room is praying all at once. During worship services, I sometimes feel like, yes, God is everywhere, but making the connection

It doesn't have to be an either/or

isn't the same when you're in a group chat with hundreds of other people. Merton probably sensed spiritual noise in the monastery despite the fact that silence was how the monks spent their days.

✓ Now I find a hopeful note in Merton's persistence in pursuing solitude. I believe he's teaching us this: when we can cultivate personal communion with the divine, it will automatically be the way we want our prayer life to be. The hunger that Merton had will draw us on. But what makes us feel connected to God in prayer? And how can we be in that prayerful state as much as possible? While access to a deeply prayerful state won't look the same for each person, we can try different things. Dip ourselves in various pools. See in which waters our souls best rise.

HOW TO SOAR

As much as Merton could feel in communion with God, and as much as he wrote about discerning God's will, I find it interesting that he had a tough time allowing the space for God to work that will. In 1947, as a thirty-two-year-old man who'd been baptized for nine years and a monk for nearly six,

willful?

✓ he notes, "I have my fingers too much in the running of my own life. . . . I put myself into God's hands, and take myself out again to readjust everything to suit my own judgment. . . . Jesus, I put myself in Your hands . . . promise to stop jumping out of Your arms to try and walk on my own feet, forgetting that I am no longer on the ground or near it! . . . Why do I mistrust Your goodness, mistrust everyone but myself,

meet every new event on the defensive, squared off against
everybody from my Superiors on down?"

Oh, Thomas. May I suggest an answer? Perhaps, because
of your cloistered existence, you haven't had enough opportunities for experiences in which you clearly see or feel God
at work in your life. You have nothing to feed your faith,
and instead you subsist on books. You're like the Hermione
Granger of Gethsemani. Hermione, one of Harry Potter's best
friends in the popular book series by J. K. Rowling, is called
"the cleverest witch of [her] age." She pushes herself to excel
in magic by studying hard. She reads loads of books, knows a
vast array of spells, and can cast them with immense focus and
power. Yet she struggles with magic that requires a more intuitive sense, such as divination or even flying on a broomstick.
When Harry tells her he's not as good at magic as she is, she
admits her magic is limited, based only on books and clever-
ness. She knows there are interior characteristics that make
a wizard powerful, characteristics she recognizes in Harry.

Thomas, you seem to sense that you are in a headspace of
too many books and too little faith. "Do not know where the
trouble lies—in too much reading and curiosity—or what?"
you write. "Not enough discipline anyway. Disciplined prayer.
The woods are not enough. Less activity (when have I said that
before?). More obscurity, more purpose, more perseverance in
the mystery of helpless prayer. More real trust in God."

Yes, too much reading. Reading does help, of course, but
one can't really learn one's way into a faith-filled trust. In fact,
it helps more to *not know* things. The poet Christian Wiman,
in his book *My Bright Abyss*, wisely observes, "Intellectuals and
artists concerned with faith tend to underestimate the radical,

inviolable innocence it requires. . . . Innocence, for the believer, remains the only condition in which intellectual truths can occur, and wonder is the precondition for all wisdom."

I'll put it this way, Thomas: you don't know how to soar. Here's what I mean.

Like you, I pray. My prayer is often an ongoing soundtrack, a conversation without ceasing. At times, it is specific and intercessory: "I am praying for . . . ," and I say the names carefully in my mind, see their faces and their beings, picture light coming their way. I see healing hands full of light, warmth, and hope laid upon them. At other times, my prayer is the corporate prayer in church or the prayers I say before I go to sleep.

But then there are times of trial, when I can sense my life is on the cusp of tremendous loss and suffering. And what do I hear in those times? Nothing. And I mean nothing, from either side. I don't feel impelled to send out words into the universe, and I feel nothing but a silent void acting as an answer. This happened the night when I lie in bed in the dark, knowing I would hear in the morning whether or not my sister Theo had overcome the infection that was shutting down her organs. In those dark hours, I could not pray.

This used to perturb me. I wondered if I had been abandoned. For my sister did die. What was I to make of the heartbreaking loss? Did the awful thing happen because God had forsaken me? I discussed this once with the rector of our church, and she told me this sense of not being able to pray was normal. She said those are the times when you have others pray for you. For a few years, I accepted her explanation. I would contact a few close friends and ask them to pray for me.

But in another of those voids of silence—this one as I stood in the hall of a New York City hospital while Katy, a dear friend I loved as a sister, underwent surgery and I waited to hear whether or not she had cancer—a realization came over me. How do I describe it? I felt like I was waiting in a quiet, open space. Then an image came to me—that of an eagle soaring. I thought of the powerful quiet of gliding through air.

I asked myself this question: What if all my previous prayers—especially the specific practices in church or in my prayer spaces at home—were the equivalent of a large bird flapping its wings in preparation for flight? Then in times of trial, when I think I cannot pray, perhaps that's when I have somehow taken off. I'm supposed to glide—be present, trust the current of air, of spirit, to uphold me so I can do what is necessary in the crisis. Gliding is silent—gliding is strong. God turns down the noise and lifts me, letting me know, *You can do this, you are not alone.* Instead of an absence of prayer, I am surrounded by prayer, effortless prayer.

But I don't know how this works, so I don't know if I can teach it. Thomas, I feel as though you would ask me if you should study aerodynamics. Should we discuss prayer in terms of drag and thrust, lift and weight? Maybe I will remind you of your words from *Conjectures of a Guilty Bystander,* about the birds who each morning "manifest themselves as birds, beginning to sing. Presently they will be fully themselves and will even fly." But in your cloistered life, you haven't been forced out of a tree to give you the chance to test your wings. You can't trust them because you haven't had the full experience of them. I suggest you only need to remember that flight is in your nature.

DISCIPLINE REQUIRED

Merton recognized his prayer life was often grounded—unable to take off, let alone soar. Though he had time alone in his hermitage, he found the quality of his prayers could still be disrupted by his own lack of focus. Just as any of us can be distracted during prayer and meditation, Merton no doubt had a lot on his mind—schemes for his next publication, communications from his friends, how much wood he needed to chop for his fire, whether the dermatitis he sometimes suffered from on his hands would ever heal.

It's like his wing-flapping was woefully ineffective and he knew it: "I realize now how weak and confused I have become—most of the time I have simply played around and daydreamed and am sadly unequipped to take a real uprooting. Hence the need of prayer and thought and discipline and the self purification."

How does one strengthen a prayer life? Maybe we can take a cue from professional athletes: quality practice. Just as they have to practice well to play well, if we cultivate a strong prayer life, we will be strong in prayer. It starts with the discipline of routine. Merton maintained the practice of praying the schedule of the Daily Office as he did in the monastery. He knew walking in the woods and being in solitude helped foster his communion with God, but he would still be subject to daydreams and distractions. In his routine, the discipline of reading his prayers aloud helped him stay on point: "Solitude—when you get saturated with silence and landscape, then you need an interior work, psalms, scripture, meditation." Note that he's talking about sacred text, not philosophy or theology. Reciting the Psalms was of particular importance to Merton. Among the belongings he left behind was a tattered copy of the Psalms in Latin, the pages so well thumbed that they are crumbling and the cover has separated from its binding.

I have to admit, for a long time I never understood the point of praying with prewritten prayers or of reciting Scripture to oneself alone in a room. Then, in 2011, I joined the Episcopal Church and learned about the *Book of Common Prayer*. The church defines the book as "a treasure chest full of devotional and teaching resources for individuals and congregations, but it is also the primary symbol of our unity." Every day, churches and individuals around the world pray the same words from this book for Sunday services, baptisms, weddings, and funerals, in addition to a Daily Office of morning, afternoon, and evening prayers.

I decided to experiment with reciting Morning Prayer daily on my own, sitting on the cushions in front of a lit candle in the small meditation space I keep in a corner of my home office. As my practice went on from days to weeks and from weeks to months, I noticed something different about my thoughts, about the material my brain happened to access in any given moment. In the same way that a song might come to me that I can hum or sing, I now had words of prayer in my mind's playlist. Instead of thinking, in a tough moment, "It'll be OK," I hear, "The Lord is good; his mercy is everlasting; and his faithfulness endures from age to age." Or I hear this, one of my favorites, when I'm getting ready for the day or to speak at an event: "Arise, shine, for your light has come, and the glory of the Lord has dawned upon you." I can't tell you how comforting it is to feel these words, like an invisible security blanket wrapped around my being.

The apostle Paul exhorted the Thessalonians to "pray without ceasing" (1 Thess 5:17). I believe walking around with words of prayer imprinted within me is a way of doing that. And I understand why it's important: Because the work of God is ongoing—creation is ongoing. I'm praying to figure out my role in that creation. A wonderful story that explains this well comes from the book *The Shack* and its film version. The story is about a man whose life and faith are shattered after the murder of his youngest child. He has an encounter with God during which he expresses his anger—really giving God what for—and demands to know why God doesn't stop bad things from happening. God, embodied by the actress Octavia Spencer, explains she doesn't make these things happen, nor does she stop them. But she is constantly working to make something of what has happened. She also wants us to know she is always here—especially when the horrific events happen. We are never alone.

Praying without ceasing reminds me of who I am and to whom I belong. And because I remember this, I can trust the air that upholds me when it's time to glide. I trust that I can soar.

PRAYING WITH ICONS

In the spring of 1968, Merton's hermitage was enlarged, with a bathroom added and, notably, a chapel. Once the construction was finished, Merton happily set about cleaning out the space and setting up an altar. Before, he'd prayed at an altar scrunched in next to his fireplace and bookcase in his front room. Now he had a dedicated space for prayer, with a tall, plain wooden rectangular block for an altar. Between two candles, Merton placed a large icon of the Madonna and Child with four smaller panels, on each an image of a saint attending them. He hung three more icons on the walls and spread out on the concrete floor a small rug with a block pattern. He writes, "My chapel is plain, bright, white-walled, bright warm red of ikons [*sic*], simplicity, light, peace."

The icons, though, had a greater function than providing the chapel with a splash of color. They were tools for prayer. The word *icon* means "image," and since the early days of Christianity, *icon* has been the name for images depicting religious stories. They can be paintings, mosaics, or enamels, and they can be large enough to cover a cathedral-sized wall or small enough to fit in a pocket. Merton's other three icons included another Madonna and Child and two icons of the prophet Elijah—one in the desert being fed by a raven and one ascending in a fiery chariot. Of the fiery Elijah, Merton writes, upon receiving it from his friend Jack Ford, "Fabulously beautiful, delicate, and strong. . . . What a thing to have in the room. It transfigures everything."

Icons are a wonderful aid for prayer, especially if a person finds that when they close their eyes to pray, their mind wanders or they fall asleep. In using an icon one prays with eyes open, focusing on the image and its story. Jim Forest, author of the book *Praying with Icons*—he was also a cofounder of the Catholic Peace Fellowship and a correspondent of Merton's in the 1960s—writes, "While prayer may often be, in Thomas Merton's words, 'like a face-to-face meeting in the dark,' cutting a major link with the physical world by closing your eyes is not a precondition of prayer. Icons help solve a very simple problem: If I am to pray with open eyes, what should I be looking at? It doesn't have to be icons, but icons are a good and helpful choice. They serve as bridges to Christ, as links with the saints, as reminders of pivotal events in the history of salvation."

Icons can be purchased in stores and online, but many people hold to the idea that an icon has to come into one's life of its own accord. The right image shows up at the right time. The Mary and four saints panels, for example, are Greek icons Merton received from writer Marco Pallis as a gift in 1965. Merton wrote to Pallis to thank him and talked about the power of the icon and its impact not only on his prayer but on the atmosphere of the little concrete-block building: "I never tire of gazing at it. There is a spiritual presence and reality about it, a true spiritual 'Thaboric' light, which seems unaccountably to proceed from the Heart of the Virgin and Child as if they had One heart, which goes out to the whole universe. It is unutterably splendid. And silent. It imposes silence on the whole hermitage."

I have four icons arranged on the small altar in my home meditation space. Though I purchased them myself, I still feel like they came to me, because learning about icons has been a gift. Our church had an interim rector who brought icons to the forefront of our congregational consciousness. She taught a class on praying with icons and even hosted sessions on how to create one, a craft known as icon writing. I was fascinated to learn that all icons depicted only very specific religious scenes, all of them from the life of Christ. For a couple of years, I'd kept on my home altar a paper copy of an image of Christ and Mary Magdalene on Easter morning in front of the empty tomb. I printed it from a photograph I'd found online. I was drawn to it by Mary's red robe, the way she was reaching out for Christ, and how the separated pieces of her hair made it look like she had dreadlocks like mine. I've always identified with Magdalene, so the image spoke to me on so many levels. In my rector's class, I learned my image was an actual icon and that I could purchase it—I did!—hand painted on wood.

If you are curious about praying with icons, I would encourage you to begin by thinking about what aspects of Christ's story speak to you. Then look up those icons and study the images. Does one connect with you more than any other? Does the image have something to offer in support of how you want to live your life?

Mary Magdalene, for example, reminds me of the quality of love and faith I want to live in the world. I'm praying for that.

I have a Madonna and Child that I found at a Coptic Christian Church in New York City and purchased because both Mary and the baby have a hint of a smile that made them seem to me very human and real. Mary reminds me of the kind of mother I want to be: strong but still capable of joy.

I also have an icon of the Annunciation, depicting the angel Gabriel telling Mary of her coming role in God's creation. I love the Magnificat, Mary's response to this news, so this icon reminds me how I feel my soul also magnifies the Lord.

My last icon, the Presentation of Christ, depicts Simeon meeting Mary and Joseph in the temple with the baby Jesus.

Simeon was a holy man who had been told by the Holy Spirit "he would not see death before he had seen the Lord's Messiah." When he sees the baby Jesus, he thanks God and declares, "My eyes have seen your salvation, which you have prepared in the presence of all peoples" (Luke 2:26, 30–31). I'm inspired by this story because it reminds me, with great hope, of how well God keeps promises.

I enjoy the powerful intentionality of praying with icons. There's also a kind of stab of delight I sense and relish, something Merton also acknowledges: "Joy before the ikon [*sic*] in the hermitage yesterday afternoon!" Suddenly prayer feels alive—like many, many good things all at once are possible. It feels like God.

THE MYSTERY OF PRAYER

I believe we focus too much on the fervent prayers that don't come through—of loved ones lost, of disappointments bitterly endured. We don't honor as much as we could the prayers that *did* come through, so quick are we to move on to the next thing we want. But when we do that, we miss out on the miracle of how deeply God wants to work in our favor—so much so that God will even answer requests we didn't make voluntarily. God seeks to fulfill every desire, even those whispered only in the deepest corners of our hearts.

About three months after my dear friend Katy died, I drove the sixty-five miles to New York City to meet with her husband and one of her childhood friends, Jillian, to go through her jewelry and her handbags, something she'd asked us to do so we would have favorite mementos of her. It was my first time in the apartment since I had seen her for the last time, the month before her passing, and it was just as hard as I thought it would be. I kept thinking, *She's not here, she's not here, she's not here.* I cried. I was really still in shock.

At first it felt unseemly to be going through her things. But soon I had the feeling that Katy would say things like "That would look good on you," and I chose a few pieces of jewelry and a couple of bags. David, Jillian, and I went to lunch at a diner down the street afterward.

When we all parted, I thought I would feel better. Instead, I felt drained and heavy, as though a wrap of lead had dropped over my shoulders. I knew this was grief, dark and weighty grief. I decided to walk back to my car, parked several blocks away, through Central Park. It was a sunny and not-so-cold day, one of those days when everyone in the city seems to be outside. The park was crowded with both residents and tourists. I took photos of the Lenten roses in bloom and a beautiful patch of red-and-gold-striped tulips.

I was thinking many things, but as I cut over to Columbus Avenue at West Seventy-Second Street, I had these two thoughts in particular. I thought about how much I love tulips but how I can't grow them in my yard because of the deer. And I thought, *This is the kind of day when you run into people you know.*

Then I thought of Jenny and how I probably would never run into her. Jenny is another dear friend, as dear as Katy. But even when we lived in the same neighborhood—the very one in which I was currently walking—I never ran into her. Now she is the executive producer of several popular television shows. At this point, she was mostly in Los Angeles and not in New York. The thought was very specific in my mind: *I will never run into Jenny.*

I had crossed Columbus and was walking down West Seventy-Third, just past Alice's Tea Cup, where I often met Katy for tea, when I heard my name. "Sophfronia!" I turned, and there she was: Jenny! A joyous meeting. We walked to a deli because she wanted a bagel. Jenny also bought a box of decorated Easter cookies for my son, Tain, and then, for me, a bunch of white tulips! "Here, you need these," she said. We talked, and we laughed. We went back to her place and talked and laughed some more before I had to leave to get back in time for the evening's Easter Vigil service.

Driving home that night, I thought about how the two things I had lamented not having were suddenly and amazingly given to me: tulips and a serendipitous visit with a close friend. I received exactly what I had needed. God had answered even though I never asked, reminding me once again of how I am well cared for. I felt humbled. I felt grace. I felt loved. God kept me from being snatched away into despair: "I am the good shepherd. I know my own and my own know me. . . . No one will snatch them out of my hand" (John 10:14, 28).

Faith is about trust, but it's also about the unexpected gift showing up in my hands, like a bunch of white tulips. Even Christ knew the importance of providing miracles, of God showing up in the world in tangible ways. But do we recognize when God does these things?

I think you needed to work on that, Thomas. "I realize how all around me are answers to prayer, as though I were living in the midst of a world that had been all made out of my prayers and needs, *in spite* of everything that went contrary to them," you write. "Yet I can live as if God were not living and praying in me! What a fool, what lack of faith!"

Prayer is a mystery, with so many paths to walk, so many branches of communication, so many pools of wonder. But it's also like you and me, Thomas, standing on the edge of one of the ponds near Gethsemani. You're pointing to a spot: dive in *there*. We just have to begin. A few years ago at my church, we began a practice called Pray First, which encouraged any group meeting to begin with prayer. It's a simple idea—after all, most people of prayer already do this, such as before a meal or, with athletes, before and after a competition. But in times of stress such as the one our church, then in a transition, was going through, we would sometimes forget to ask for guidance before delving into our work.

I decided to do the same thing. Instead of waiting for a prayer to surface involuntarily in my consciousness, I began actively reminding myself to pray first: before teaching a class, before speaking at an event, before driving my son to school. This practice encouraged me to pray for everything—the fellowships and residencies I apply for, my writing, my students, my relationships, my travels. Again, prayer without ceasing. I know I must stay close to God. As Frederick Buechner writes, "Go where your best prayers take you. Unclench the fists of your spirit and take it easy. Breathe deep of the glad air and live one day at a time. Know that you are precious."

Diligent, but with unclenched fists: perhaps this is the remedy to heal the Hermione in all of us.

9

Hopeful Eyes on a Hopeless Issue

HOW TO RESIST RACISM

We discover that belief in the Negro as a person is accepted only with serious qualifications, while the notion that he is to be treated as Christ has been overlooked.

I WANT TO TALK TO THOMAS MERTON ABOUT RACE. OF course one might doubt whether a cloistered white man who lived in Kentucky in the middle part of the last century would have anything useful to offer, but this particular monk knew that such a conversation is never about race alone. Talking about race means, among many things, sharing our fears and frustrations about our place in the world, about how people are treated, about a hope for better opportunities that never seem to materialize. In other words, it's about dignity, respect, a shared humanity, and ultimately, our hearts and souls. Racism is not just about white people treating people of color badly; it is about how the repercussions of that treatment reverberate for everyone, to the detriment of us all.

This was the very high level of Merton's thinking about race. It goes well beyond "love your neighbor as yourself" Christian behavior, so I don't believe one can attach his thoughts solely to his conversion to Catholicism. There is something so intuitive about Merton's views that I think talking to him about race would be helpful. I have a hunch that he, unlike many white people, would be willing to go to the heart of the matter of race, and in a way that doesn't focus on him.

Merton moved to the United States in the late 1930s, when African Americans were referred to as "Negroes" and segregation was a fact of life. His own position—that of a young white man and a Columbia University student—was a privileged one that would have allowed him, if he chose, to ignore the injustice and inequality imposed on people of color. He could have looked at society's status quo and taken it in an "it is what it is" or "this is how things are done" kind of way. But somehow he was able to look at race and say, quite coherently, that something was very wrong. When he was a teacher at St. Bonaventure's College in Upstate New York, he met Catherine de Hueck, a woman who had visited the school to speak about the conditions in Harlem and of the community center she ran there called Friendship House. Merton asked her afterward if he could come to Harlem and volunteer. She agreed, and he arrived via subway on a rain-soaked, humid day in August 1941. His impression of Harlem affected him so deeply that he would recall it with stunning power years later in *The Seven Storey Mountain*:

Here in this huge, dark, steaming slum, hundreds of thousands of Negroes are herded together like cattle, most of them with nothing to eat and nothing to do. All the senses and imagination and sensibilities and emotions and sorrows and desires and hopes and ideas of a race with vivid feelings and deep emotional reactions are forced in upon themselves, bound inward by an iron ring of frustration: the prejudice that hems them in with its four insurmountable walls. In this huge cauldron, inestimable natural gifts, wisdom, love, music, science, poetry are stamped down and left to boil with the dregs of an elementally corrupted nature, and thousands upon thousands of souls are destroyed by vice and misery and degradation, obliterated, wiped out, washed from the register of the living, dehumanized. . . . Harlem is there by way of a divine indictment against New York City and the people who live downtown and make their money downtown. The brothels of Harlem, and all its prostitution, and its dope-rings, and all the rest are the mirror of the polite divorces and the manifold cultured adulteries of Park Avenue: they are God's commentary on the whole of our society.

He would return many times and would perform various tasks while at Friendship House. He looked after children, led prayer services, sorted through clothing donations. He thought seriously of making Friendship House his own life's work and went back and forth trying to decide whether to live in poverty serving God in Harlem or to live in poverty serving God as a monk in Kentucky. He eventually chose the cloistered existence.

Once he entered the monastery, Merton wrote little about race other than the Harlem passages in his autobiography.

But those pages were enough for the leaders of the civil rights movement to mark him as an ally. When he took up the subject again years later—writing essays such as "The Black Revolution: Letters to a White Liberal" in 1963 and books like *Seeds of Destruction* in 1964 as the civil rights movement gained steam—Merton came to the table with credibility, with what now would be called "street cred." In a 2019 article on Merton's civil rights writing, Dr. Gregory K. Hillis of Bellarmine University, which houses the Merton Center, summarizes the Black revolution essay: "Overarching the entire essay is Merton's conviction that the oppression of African Americans is systemic and that white liberals (a) do not do enough to fight against the racism baked into American society; and (b) are, in fact, guilty of propping up this racist system for their own well-being." Hillis also points out how one noted reviewer basically said Merton didn't know what he was talking about only to turn around, years later, and say that not only did he regret the review but "what bothers me now is the degree of accuracy in your predictions and prophecies in general."

Eldridge Cleaver, the founder of the Black Panther Party, notes in his autobiography *Soul on Ice* how he would often reread Merton's Harlem pages in the autobiography whenever he felt his resolve weakening. The passages helped him "to become once more a rigid flame of indignation." Merton met with Black students from Louisville who were on retreat at the abbey so that he could learn more. Dr. Hillis, in his article, quotes one man who said he carried one of Merton's books in his pocket when crossing the Edmund Pettis Bridge in Selma in 1965. A Black woman he quotes said she "felt alienated by her church and religious community for her civil rights work in the 1960s," but "Merton got it when few others did."

Sounds like I've come to the right monk for this conversation.

Yet I don't want to be a rigid flame of indignation. That seems to me to be a tough way to go through the world, especially since flames can burn out eventually. I want instead a way of resisting racism so that I don't become what I behold. I don't want my life weighed down by anger, hopelessness, and resentment. How do I do that, Thomas? How do I do that when the racism you wrote about is still prevalent but is now covered in a patina that makes people think mistakenly that the years have worn it down?

Here's what's on my mind. I have a biracial teenage son growing up in a time when it's not uncommon to see videos on the internet and the evening news of unarmed Black people being shot and killed. Tain has his own strong faith and a sunny disposition that makes him look for, and see, the best in all he beholds. I feel the need to affirm his attitude, but I also have to be real with him. I must be vigilant about knowledge—and through knowledge, protection. When he was about eight or nine and decided to don a black choir robe, a cross, and a purple stole in order to be Dr. Martin Luther King Jr. for our church's All Saints' Day procession, he told me why he chose Dr. King: he was a great leader and helped Black people have better lives. I was so proud of him, but I also knew I had to guide him that despite appearances, including having a Black president in office for most of Tain's young life, Dr. King's fight was not over.

I don't want Tain to become fearful and angry. Yes, the content of his character is important, and he knows to be kind and helpful to others. But he also has to be aware, now that he's grown lanky and well past the six-foot mark, of how others may view him. He has fair skin, dark-brown eyes, and a few freckles sprinkled over his cheeks. His dark-brown hair, once worn short and close-cropped, is now long and curly, topping his head like a soft cloud. It's the hair we often talk about. Tain needs to understand the possible effects of having such hair.

I've shown him pictures of Malcolm Gladwell, the best-selling author of books like *Blink* and *The Tipping Point*, and we've discussed a 2011 CNN interview in which Gladwell spoke of a time when he let his hair grow longer, with surprising results. "I'm of mixed race," he said, "and the minute I began to look more like people's stereotype of a black male, with a big Afro, I got stopped by police, and when I went through customs at the airport, I would always get pulled out. I was getting speeding tickets left and right; it was really kind of a striking transformation in the way the world viewed me. Even though I was exactly the same person, once I had longer hair the world saw me as being profoundly different."

Something like this may happen to Tain. We look at images on television and in magazines and discuss how African Americans are portrayed. I remind him to pull back the hood of his jacket from his head when he walks into a store. I showed him footage of NFL player Michael Bennett being apprehended during an active shooting situation simply because, being tall and Black, he stood out as a threat. When Tain learns to drive, I will teach him how to behave during a police stop, how to keep his hands in view and make no sudden moves.

I still think about the 2015 video showing a Black man, Walter Scott, who had been stopped for a traffic violation. We see him as he is being gunned down by a police officer. He is running away when the white officer fires eight shots at his back. Scott falls face down, and the officer handcuffs him that way. The officer does not check to see if he is breathing. He does not turn him over. He tosses a Taser near the man's body. Later, he will claim that Scott had tried to take it from him. Scott receives no assistance, not even from the Black officer who later arrives on the scene. Scott dies at the scene. The coroner will later say that Scott was struck five times. Walter Scott was unarmed.

Sitting outdoors in Minneapolis on an April day, I discuss the video with a friend. We talk about the shock of witnessing the killing, of watching Walter Scott fall, of the bitter taste forced in our mouths after seeing him hit the ground. What really leaves our souls scorched and grieving is the casual behavior of the police officer who fires the weapon. It's as though this event were not extraordinary for him. It's as though he has no sense of the impact of his action, the fact that he has just ripped a precious life from the world.

It's this sense of my soul being scorched that I need to heal, Thomas. I don't want to pass it on to my son.

WORDS OF ADVICE

In 1963, Merton met a young Black priest, August Thompson, who visited Gethsemani from his home parish in Alexandria, Louisiana. A few months later, Thompson wrote to Merton for guidance after Thompson had been berated by his bishop for speaking out on the poor treatment of Black people in the Catholic Church: How they could only receive communion after whites had already received it. How white Catholics would rather pay someone to drive a Black Catholic to another town for church than have the person attend in their parish. How Thompson himself was prohibited from saying Mass at white parishes and how some white Catholics refused to call him "Father." The church—a place that should have offered solace and compassion—instead betrayed its Black congregants and all notions of Christian love by only giving them more of what they experienced daily in the secular world.

It's striking to me that the advice you gave him, Thomas, appealed to the priest's loving heart and not his indignant mind. You instructed him to handle his bishop's disapproval with compassion toward the bishop. "You have to take into account the absolute blindness and absolute self-righteousness of people who have been scooled [*sic*] by centuries of prejudice and injustice to see things their way and no other," you write. To tell you the truth, Thomas, I would have taken this as condescending words from an out-of-touch white monk. It sounds like you're telling him—along with the white moderates of the day—"Be patient; don't ask for too much; change happens slowly." But I realize I need to be patient with the words in your response and understand that what you were trying to do for Thompson is what I need to do for myself. You wanted him to take care of his heart first. If he kept bashing himself against the stone wall of the bishop's blind racism, it would only lead to Thompson's disillusionment, and then anger and pain. But if he led with a loving heart, he could instead seep into the stone, like water trickling down a mountain, and eventually crack the mountain open from within, all without compromising his own emotional health. You sought to teach Thompson the essence of nonviolence.

Having studied Mahatma Gandhi's philosophy of nonviolent protest, you read and taught to your novices Martin Luther King Jr.'s "Letter from a Birmingham Jail." You learned that nonviolence is not only a way of protest but a way of being, that if one is careless in thoughts and words, one can be violent without realizing it.

"Where minds are full of hatred and where imaginations dwell on cruelty, torment, punishment, revenge and death, then inevitably there will be violence and death," you write. This tells me that if I want to escape anger and hopelessness, my focus shouldn't be on the wrongs being done. I have to begin with my humanity and understanding my truth. When you were studying Gandhi, you wrote, "I need to understand and practice non-violence in every way. It is because my life is not firmly based on the truth that I am morally in confusion and in captivity—under the half truths and prejudices that rule others and rule me through them."

I could be ruled by what I see—the ongoing occurrences of racism and hate crimes and the long shadow of police shootings of unarmed Black men. In order to release the power of these instances over my mind and heart, it is imperative that I unravel some of the complicated threads within myself.

A SENSE OF BETRAYAL

What does rule me? Perhaps an immortal wound. The writer Robert Vivian once lectured on how we all have immortal wounds: events in our lives we simply cannot get over. The writer James Baldwin, author of provocative works such as *Notes of a Native Son* and *The Fire Next Time*, never got over his stepfather's ruthless abuse or the racism that made him leave the United States and live in Europe. These wounds showed up in everything he wrote. Vivian was saying that if we understood our wounds, we would understand what makes our writing unique.

I have a wound about betrayal. And the betrayal wasn't even my own.

I was eleven years old when the miniseries *Roots: The Saga of an American Family* aired on television. I remember being fascinated by the friendship between the enslaved girl Kizzy and the slaveowner's daughter, Missy Anne. Missy Anne teaches Kizzy how to read—maybe this was the source of my fascination, because I loved to read. I didn't understand, though, how this went against the law of the time and how dire the consequences were. After Kizzy writes a note for a slave trying to escape, her skill is discovered and she is sold. She is put on a cart, and as her new owner prepares to haul her away, Kizzy is screaming for Missy Anne.

The scream cut me so deeply that I looked up the scene in Alex Haley's novel, which inspired the televised series and is closely based on the history of Haley's ancestors. In those pages, I noted the repeated letters and capitalizations. It looked something like MISSSSY ANNNEEEE!!!

I kept waiting for Missy Anne to appear—to say something, if only good-bye, to her friend. When she didn't come, I assumed she wasn't at home or had been put someplace in the house where she couldn't hear Kizzy. But then the scene cuts to Missy Anne, sitting calmly despite the screams. She coolly observes how stupid Kizzy had been. And that was it. I couldn't believe the betrayal, the bonds of friendship torn asunder. I wondered if the bond had ever been real in the first place.

My disappointments and uncomfortable interactions around race usually involve strangers: The supermarket cashier who doesn't realize my white husband and I are together. The person in an elevator who thinks it's OK to touch my dreadlocks. Betrayals, to me anyway, are about people who are supposed to know you. They intentionally put you in a place of having to be something other than yourself. Maybe I'm careful now to allow people close to me who are unlikely to harbor betrayal—as if I can really tell! But that doesn't mean the wound is not at work within me.

In 2015, my brother's home in Florida was spray-painted with a racist threat. I posted on social media the photo of the ugly black lettering, dripping down a wall on the side of his house, as I wanted people to know racism was active and affecting someone you know. One friend started a GoFundMe campaign to raise funds to have my brother's house painted, a campaign that ended up earning more than the goal amount.

But a good number of my white friends were simply stunned. They were surprised that this kind of thing still happens, and they shared the post with equal amounts of shock and horror. The Black Lives Matter movement was already going strong at that point. And the spray-painting happened only weeks after a young white man, Dylann Roof, shot and killed nine African Americans during a prayer group at the Emanuel African Methodist Episcopal Church in Charleston, South Carolina. I wanted to ask, "What country are you living in?" I thought they should know better. It may not be a betrayal, but it feels awfully close.

THE COLOR OF FAITH

The deeper truth, though, is that the question "What country are you living in?" doesn't help—it's essentially resentment, not compassion. It's this kind of thinking Merton wanted Thompson to avoid when he advised him about his bishop. If he could focus on nonviolence, then Thompson had a better chance of achieving something greater. In parsing Merton's guidance, author Hillis said Merton was actually "calling Thompson to work for his bishop's conversion." White religious leaders need to be converted too, a lesson we continue to learn. And the way to do it is through listening and understanding—a conversation and not a contentious battle. "Merton was a great proponent of dialogue, which he understood to be central to the task of nonviolence," Hillis said.

Conversion? Thomas, are you telling me the race issue is really an issue of faith? I'm willing to explore that. You say the purpose of such nonviolent conversation is then to "awaken the conscience of the white man to the awful reality of his injustice . . . so that he will be able to see that the Negro problem is really a *white* problem: that the cancer of injustice and hate which is eating white society and is only partly manifested in racial segregation with all its consequences, *is rooted in the heart of the white man himself.*"

But what is fruitful dialogue? And where is it to be found? The dialogue I've experienced, to my frustration, hasn't gone

anywhere near an awakening of conscience. When the Black
Lives Matter movement first came to the forefront, I attended
diversity conversations that never seemed to get to a dis-
cussion of the current situation. That would have required
dialogue on questions such as, What is going on right now?
What types of racism do we see being enacted these days in
our streets, workplaces, and churches? How do we listen to—
or keep out—the voices that are telling us that racism is alive
and well? But the people who shared in the conversations in
which I participated—most of them white—preferred to speak
instead about "what *was*." They told stories of what they had
done, how they had participated in the civil rights movement,
how they had attended protests and rallies and how, yes, the
Jim Crow era was terrible, but compared to that, things are so
much better now. As well-meaning as they were, their words
eventually began to sound like the trope "I have Black friends."

What do I want to hear instead? I guess something along
these lines, which you wrote in 1967: "I face the fact that I am
living in an immoral, blind, even in some sense criminal society which is hypocritical, bloated, self-righteous, and unable
to see its true condition—by and large the people are 'nice'
as long as they are not disturbed in their comfortable and
complacent lives. They cannot see the price of their 'respect-
ability.' And I am part of it and I don't know what to do about
it—apart from symbolic and futile gestures."

If I heard that, I think I would respond, "I don't know what
to do either. But the fact that we're here in this same place of
not knowing is a really good place to start." From there we
could explore processes that both look at the bigger picture
and also challenge us as individuals to make change from

within. Your reading of James Baldwin's *The Fire Next Time* and *Nobody Knows My Name* informed your view of the big picture, a view that is still relevant:

> He [Baldwin] seems to know exactly what he is talking about, and his statements are terribly urgent. One of the things that makes most sense—an application of the ideas behind non-violence, but I think it is absolutely true: that the sit-in movement is not just to get the negroes a few hamburgers, it is for the sake of the white people, and for the country. He is one of the few genuinely concerned Americans, one whose concern I can really believe. The liberation of the Negroes is necessary for the liberation of the whites and for their recovery of a minimum of self-respect, and reality. Above all he makes very shrewd and pointed statements about the futility and helplessness of white liberals who sympathize but never do anything. Well, a few have got beat up on freedom rides, this is true. But really the whole picture is pitiful. A scene of helplessness, inertia, stupidity, erosion.

There is a risk when, as we work on our individual responses to racism, we put front and center the picture that Merton and Baldwin describe. It goes against the popular "things are getting better" view to the point where we might become the child in the fairy tale "The Emperor's New Clothes": the innocent truth-teller who doesn't realize that by shouting out that the emperor is really naked, he is toppling the secure structure of his community. Thomas, at times I feel like the child you reference when you write, "Our vocation, as innocent bystanders—and the very condition of our terrible innocence—is to do what the child did, and keep on saying the king is naked, at the cost of being condemned criminals."

If we don't become the truth-tellers, then a different kind of erosion can happen in which resentment breeds, a resentment that would threaten the wholeness of my heart and soul. If nothing else, I must be whole and respond to racism in a way that is true to the depths of my being. What does that look like?

We're getting on the same page, I think, Thomas, because something else you observed does give me hope. You wrote, "These Negroes are not simply judging the white man and rejecting him. On the contrary, they are seeking by Christian love and sacrifice to redeem him, to enlighten him, so as not only to save his soul from perdition, but also to awaken his mind and conscience."

SEEDS OF REDEMPTION

Redemption. Yes. My friend and neighbor Jane, after reading my first novel, a story about a family dealing with drug addiction, said that I seem to be "all about redemption." She added, "You don't throw people away."

I suppose redemption works in me, to the good, so deeply that I don't always recognize when I'm doing it. I'm drafting a novel about an enslaved girl who is of mixed race and a white girl. They are half sisters who share a father, a slave owner. As I work my way through figuring out the plot, developing the characters, and considering their actions, it occurred to me that, yet again, I have Kizzy and Missy Anne on my mind.

I am seeking to redeem Missy Anne, writing still from this immortal wound.

Is this my way of rebelling, Thomas? It seems so small and meaningless. Perhaps we are in the same position—feeling as though we have no way to exert significant influence on a pressing issue. But we can respond with what we do best: write. We put words out into the world, scatter them like seeds in the great hope they can become something more—something not destructive. You would tell me just write—just write, and make sure it's good. I think this works for me, because as I read over my pages and see how I'm righting wrongs in my fictional worlds, I see how I'm accessing the compassion you speak of.

And because I can access it, I can offer and model it for my son. In turn, he supports my hope. Already he's showing me the possibilities. I drive him forty-five minutes to school and, depending on traffic, nearly an hour home each day so that he can attend an arts high school in an urban area. He studies theater and enjoys a more diverse environment in terms of race, class, and sexual orientation than we have where we live. He and his friends are so accepting of each other that even if they don't know someone's gender, they don't ask.

They only care about the person: what their name is, the activities they favor, how they are doing on any given day. I think about this attitude blossoming throughout Tain's generation and the generations to come. It makes me feel an abundance of hope.

10

Swiping Right in the Marketplace

HOW TO LOVE

To say that I am made in the image of God is to say that love is the reason for my existence, for God is love. Love is my true identity. Selflessness is my true self. Love is my true character. Love is my name.

THE EARLY MONTHS OF 1966 HELD SEVERAL BLEAK aspects for Merton. In January, he learned a friend from his young New York City days had died of a heart attack. His own health was poor—his hands would go numb to the point where holding a pen was difficult, and when he learned that the numbness stemmed from vertebrae problems that would require major back surgery in March, he called the news "a kind of defeat." In these pages of his journal, he is wrapped up in thoughts of growing older and of death. Before leaving for the hospital, he listens to the church bell tolling in the dark and writes, "Yet I know I have to die sometime and may this not all be the beginning of it?" He expressed gratitude for his hermitage and finally having a life of solitude there. He ends the entry with the words "There are greater gifts even than this and God knows best what is for my good—and for the good of the whole world. The best is what He wills."

If "the best is what He wills" is true, then by this assess-ment, it seems the best God saw for Merton was to have his world completely rocked to the core. He did go to the hospital, and he did undergo a successful back surgery. And then? A young student nurse was assigned to oversee his rehabilitation—and during the following weeks, they fell in love. One month later, while recuperating back at the mon-astery, he made forbidden calls from the monastery to the young woman he referred to in his journal as "M." Just one month removed from his thoughts of death and ill health, Merton writes, "All I know is that I love her so much I can hardly think of anything but her. Also I know that in itself this love is a thing of enormous value (never has anyone given herself to me so completely, so openly, so frankly, and never have I responded so completely!). Yet it is in absolute conflict with every social canon, feeling, predetermination etc. And *everyone*, the pious and the feisty, will use it for one thing only—to crush and discredit us."

Even though I knew about Merton's relationship with M. before encountering his journals, reading those words inspired mind-boggling delight. When I think of how dour and dark Merton had been only a few weeks before, this amazing turnaround certainly demonstrated the power—perhaps even the divine power—of love. He is giddy and boyish, defiant and joyful, even focused and prayerful all at once. And yet he saw all of these changes as making perfect sense: "Clearly this love is not a contradiction of my solitude but a mysterious part of it. It fits strangely and without conflict into my inner life of meditation and prayer. . . . But it fits also into my own way of emptiness and unknowing, and indeed my moments of inner silence are my main source of strength, light, and love—along with my Mass which is most ardent these days and in which I feel most closely united with her in Christ."

Merton also recognized a transformation of his own romantic heart, from that of a young man who enjoyed the company of women but couldn't trust whether any of the girls he dated—and one assumes this includes the one he impregnated in England—really cared for him, to that of a mature soul accepting that he could be truly beloved. I'm guessing his youthful mistrust was a reflection of his own feelings; he probably knew how flimsy his level of commitment was, so he didn't expect theirs to be any different. The previous year, on his fiftieth birthday, Merton had reflected on his past indiscretions and came to the following conclusion: "I suppose I regret most my lack of love, my selfishness and glibness (covering a deep shyness and need of love) with girls who, after all, did love me I think, for a time. My great fault was my inability really to believe it, and my effort to get complete assurance and perfect fulfillment. So one thing on my mind is sex, as something I didn't use maturely and well, something I gave up without having come to terms with it."

So the miracle with M. was not only that she loved him but that he was both strong enough to accept her love and vulnerable enough to return it. And though Merton never consummated his relationship with M., his love of her somehow allowed a kind of reconciliation of Merton to his physical being. "Instead of feeling impure I feel purified," he says. "I feel that somehow my sexuality has been made real and decent again after years of rather frantic suppression (for though I thought I had it all truly controlled, this was an illusion.) I feel less sick, I feel human, I am grateful for her love which is so totally mine."

integration ? ✓

It's fascinating that while he was in the hold of this love, Merton knew it was important to document it, both for himself and for her. He wrote poems for M. and even wrote a lengthy diary entry to tell the story of their love, entitled *A Midsummer Diary for M.*, which he fashioned as a book and delivered to her in person. The wonderful result of this diligence is that Merton, by examining himself in love, can, in a way that one wouldn't expect of a hermit monk, teach us plenty about how to love:

> I can see that it is going to go like this now with questioning, anguish, moments of passion, joy, then more anguish. Better settle down wisely and peacefully to a long struggle in which ✓ we sweat out our passion and (if possible) simmer down to a peaceful, loving, lasting friendship that will sustain our affection for years to come. That is what we both want. I must really pray for wisdom and guidance. But I *do* love her deeply. Actually, as I wrote her today, the only answer is *sacrifice*. If we are willing to love each other in a spirit of true sacrifice, our love will endure and deepen and will be consecrated by God. If we fail, our love will soon be lying in ruins and we will both be very hurt, frustrated and ashamed. My objective now should be *to prevent this happening* at all costs!

If Merton and M. had been able to shape the relationship into the lasting, loving friendship he hopes for in the entry, they probably would have found space in each other's lives and realized a shape for their love that would have provided some comfort: *anam cara*, the soul friend of which poet and philosopher John O'Donohue wrote.

If Merton could have been restrained and low-key, perhaps he and M. could have settled into a routine of regular correspondence and an in-person meeting once a year. Maybe we would have found their full correspondence among his papers and could have learned what a spiritual friendship looked like. But of course he couldn't be wise. Merton's personality didn't handle anguish very well. He pushed the envelope, insisting his friends help him and M. to see each other and making the calls he knew he shouldn't be making from the monastery office.

By the middle of June, one of the monks had reported him. After that, any connection with M. was next to impossible, because he wasn't allowed to receive her letters, nor could he call her unless a friend drove him to a pay phone. This moved him to "all or nothing" terms, especially in M.'s eyes. But he knew he couldn't give up the hermitage. Not even for her. Not for the outside world. In *A Midsummer Diary for M.*, he wrote, "M. is . . . in the end saying that I should leave it all behind and settle for love. But at this stage of the game, to face the absurdity of life in this other form is much too complicated for me. I have lost any ability to hope in that kind of happiness, because as soon as love gets fixed, stabilized (as society wants it to be), then it commands its own battery of fictions and illusions. One would have to pretend something else, something more complicated even than what I try to avoid pretending now."

They could have chosen to do that!

I wish Thomas and M. had had someone on their side to talk to, if only to explore fully the possibility of a marriage. Those who knew Merton seemed more concerned about his reputation than about his emotional longings. I don't know why I wish this for them. I suppose I feel there would have been more power in making their own choice about the relationship instead of having it made for them by a situation that dictated that he not be in the relationship at all. My heart hurts for them both.

LESSONS IN LOVE

Merton recognized the value of his experience with love and the value created in him because he had loved. I'm impressed by the fact that he wanted to write about love and that he didn't seem to care how strange it must have looked to be a monk addressing the topic. But it was more important for him to articulate what can happen when we can avail ourselves properly of love—how the love radiating from us and reaching other people can become something else, something transcendent. Merton was beginning to grasp this in October 1966 when, his affair with M. over, he was reading the notebooks of the French Algerian writer Albert Camus and quoting them in his own journal: "When you have once seen the glow of happiness on the face of a beloved person, you know that a man can have no other vocation than to awaken that light on the faces surrounding him."

Merton comments, "It is one of the most beautiful passages in all Camus and so well expresses my own deepest belief. One of the things that best justifies my coming to Gethsemani is the 'light' I have seen on her face when we have been happy together—and the happiness that others had too because I am here. And what about my own happiness because she is who she is and she is there?"

You knew your own happiness, Thomas, because although loving M. upended your life and caused you enormous frustration and embarrassment, you also felt joy. You emerged from the experience a changed man and wrote from that perspective, in the hope of sharing what you had learned. I like that we can have this conversation—that you could come away from an experience in which you'd been immature, giddy, perhaps even kind of crazy, to discuss and not deny the glory of love and how it connects us to God. I'm not sure I would otherwise have had patience with your work. Maybe I would have had a touch of suspicion.

But to write bravely of the reality of love and its power? That's everything. And you did it.

THE "SWIPE-RIGHT" MARKETPLACE

Before the end of 1966, Merton had published an essay called "A Buyer's Market for Love?" (This was later published in the book *Love and Living* as "Love and Need: Is Love a Package or a Message?") While he would go on to write other pieces about love, this one speaks best to what love has become in our current society—an ongoing quest that takes us outside of ourselves and into a realm that Merton referred to as a market where we trade in love, looking for the best deal possible.

I want someone to love me. Whenever I read or hear someone say that, I picture a person stripped bare, standing with palms up, the essence of vulnerability. The image is breathtaking in its beauty, frightening in its truth. I think we all walk around like that inside. We clothe ourselves to hide the shame of this want. Some go even further—they put on armor. And they continue, layer after layer, until no one can see or even sense the light glowing from their vulnerability. They hide what makes them lovable, all the while claiming to want love. They put themselves on the market, a place where, as Merton writes, "love is regarded as a deal. . . . In order to make a deal you have to appear in the market with a worthwhile product. . . . We unconsciously think of ourselves as objects for sale on the market."

When we begin to think of ourselves as objects for sale, Merton writes, "we come to consider ourselves and others not as *persons* but as *products*—as 'goods.' . . . We size each other up and make deals with a view to our own profit. We do not give ourselves in love, we make a deal that will enhance our own product and therefore no deal is final. Our eye is already on the next deal and this next deal need not necessarily be with the same customer. Life is more interesting when you make a lot of deals with a lot of new customers."

I wonder what Thomas would say if I could tell him this market is now digital and breathtakingly fast. In the seconds it takes to swipe right or swipe left in a dating app, multiple deals can be made. But the swipe-right culture makes us too quick to discard, too quick to judge. The level of heartbreak and deceit in these arenas is turned up to deafening levels. Thomas puts it more succinctly—we are also judging and, in a way, discarding ourselves in this process: "We cannot help revising our estimate of the deal we have made. We cannot help going back on it and making a 'better' deal with someone else who is more satisfying. . . . [This behavior] has disastrous affects [*sic*], for it leads people to manipulate each other for selfish ends."

What is the value of love in this marketplace? It's hard to tell. Love doesn't seem to be the product of interest anymore. And those in the marketplace may not stay with a deal long enough to recognize the value of the change that love can bring into their lives. Because, really, they think they don't need transformation. At their basest level—and this is what Merton himself noticed—our egos depend not on the value we attach to love but on our own valuation in the marketplace. The higher number of deals possible, we think, the lesser the chance of being hurt or even deeply affected by love's sting. So we count the number of texts. We count the number of dates. The fact that we're talking in numbers makes it more of a game, so we don't have to take it seriously. "Today, one's security and one's identity have to be constantly reaffirmed: nothing is permanent, everything is in movement," Merton writes. "You have to move with it. You have to come up with something new each day. Every morning you have to prove that you are still there. You have to keep making deals."

A RETURN TO LOVE

How do we escape the whirl of the marketplace? Turn off the app. Take off the armor. To love is to be vulnerable. You have to be willing to fall, and such willingness takes intention. Merton reflected that love is not something that just happens to you. He writes, "Our English expression 'to fall in love' suggests an unforeseen mishap that may or may not be fatal.... It reflects a peculiar attitude toward love and toward life itself—a mixture of fear, awe, fascination, and confusion."

But so many people try to be cool and collected and not fall in love—or at least not admit it first. They play love as a big game of "Gotcha!" and are unwilling to say the words "I love you" just in case the sentiment isn't returned. Most of them can't win, though, because, as Merton writes, "the [person] who is constantly seeking an object worthy of love and constantly rejecting every object because he still wants to find one that is *really worthy* is perhaps in the end only pretending to seek and pretending only in order to dissimulate his own complete lack of love. For if one has love in him he will soon find an object worthy of love and will be able to love everyone and everything."

Love is an expression of who we are within ourselves. This expression has value regardless of how it is received (or not) in the marketplace. Our capacity to love tells us who we really are. Why else would love show up as prominently as it does in the Bible, in both Old and New Testaments? If, by Jesus's commandment to love one another, God is calling us to it, then love must be vital. Merton writes, "He who loves is more alive and more real than he was when he did not love. That is perhaps why love seems dangerous: the lover finds in himself too many new powers, too many new insights. When a person is undergoing that kind of inner cataclysm, anything might happen. And thank God, it does happen. The world would not be worth much if it didn't!"

FORGIVING YOURSELF

I would add this: because love comes from within us, love has to be present within ourselves before we can give it away. Christ taught us to love our neighbors as ourselves. Here's the thing, though. Our big hurdle is in the "as ourselves" part—loving our neighbors *as ourselves*. We have to develop the sense or, more accurately, the belief that we are worthy of love. When self-love is missing, not only can we not give love, but we expect others to make up for the shortfall. We expect someone or something else—whether a person, a pet, a job, a vacation, a new car—to complete us. No one can fill that kind of void. And it's unfair to ask for that kind of lopsided commitment. If you don't love yourself, you also put yourself at risk: so many people have stayed in abusive relationships because they didn't have the self-esteem to leave.

If you can develop your own sense of validation, you are no longer dependent on the marketplace to provide it. You no longer size up people you see in the world as potential partners, nor are you concerned about them sizing you up. A calm opens up that allows you to simply be yourself. Suddenly, love can flow naturally from your being. It's not withheld or dammed up to be wielded as currency.

Getting to this place of calm and acceptance, I believe, starts with forgiveness. When someone speaks words that prove they don't like themselves, I think they are responding to a shadow of reproof for past wrongs. Just as Merton often berated himself for his reckless behavior as a young man, for careless words and thoughts, and even for not being productive enough in his solitude, so many of us do the same. There's a flow of "I'm a terrible person. I did this; I didn't do that."

I eat poorly.

I don't read enough.

I'm a thoughtless friend (or child or coworker).

I'm a bad parent.

I'm lazy.

This is where to start—forgive yourself. Offer forgiveness to yourself for your petty annoyances, for being yourself at your most disconnected, and for being what you think is unlovable. Then prepare yourself. Remember, you've just recognized all the parts of your flawed, imperfect, sublimely human nature. What makes you believe love can be anything other than just as messy? Quite messy. Don't be afraid of the messiness.

What makes for a good love story? We usually think, "Does the story have a happy ending?" How the love got to the happy ending is irrelevant. All that matters is that the couple "in love" ends up together. But that isn't always the case, as some of the best love stories of our time tell us. Think *Casablanca*. Think *Love Story*. And yes, think Merton's relationship with M. The best love stories stick with you because they are not really about the stories of the couples. They are stories of love. A good love story will offer up all the truth of love, acknowledging everything that a whole and living love actually is: messy, complicated, frustrating, exhilarating, life changing. The best love stories acknowledge the imperfection, the brokenness of love. In one of my favorite films, *Moonstruck*, the lovelorn baker Johnny Cammareri (Nicolas Cage) has it exactly right: "Love doesn't make things easy.

It breaks our hearts; it's messy. We're here to love all the wrong people and die. The storybooks are bulls*#!."

We have to trust that the messiness was all worth it. And maybe, as Merton writes in the wake of his relationship with M., something even more: "Was I being faithful in an obscure way to some other and more inscrutable call that was from God? Somehow I can't help believing that I was. The conviction won't leave me. For that very reason—I must never let the same thing happen with any other woman, for if my love for M. and hers for me is from Him, then there can be no 'others.'"

I think of the line in the film *Bohemian Rhapsody* where Mary, the lifelong friend of Queen's lead singer, Freddie Mercury, tells the singer he doesn't need to be afraid of being alone—that he is loved by her, his bandmates, his family. "It's enough," she says to him.

I hear those words even more deeply now. I wonder if somehow, Thomas, you came to the same calculation. The love of your monastery brothers, of your friends near and far, of a woman whose love you received and returned: perhaps you added it all up and decided, "It's enough."

In Sight of the Harbor
MEETING DEATH WITHOUT FEAR

*Death is someone you see very clearly with eyes in the
center of your heart: eyes that see not by reacting to
light, but by reacting to a kind of a chill from within
the marrow of your own life.*

THIS THOMAS MERTON QUOTATION SHOWS UP ON REFRIG-
erator magnets and online compendiums of quotations. It is
available to be plucked out whenever someone wants a few
pithy words about death. It's often tagged as "inspirational."
My best guess is that people like it because it expresses a cold,
clear courage with the calm of a frosty winter sky. It's how
someone would want to face death—no fear, no regret, only
a cool recognition of the inevitable.

But none of these quote mills cite where these words can
be found in Merton's writing, and they don't provide crucial
context. Merton was writing of a time when he was only seventeen, gravely sick from a blood infection, and how the death
he saw so closely drifting past his bedside was his own. This
was before he had faith, when he believed in nothing. Maybe

his adolescent self thought dying could be his way of giving the world his middle finger. "And I lay there with nothing in my heart but apathy," he writes. "There was a kind of pride and spite in it: as if it was life's fault that I had to suffer a little discomfort, and for that I would show my scorn and hatred of life, and die, as if that were a revenge of some sort. . . . If I have to die—what of it. What do I care? Let me die, then, and I'm finished."

Merton processed death differently because he had lost his parents so young, making his scorn understandable. At seventeen he was already an orphan. His father had succumbed to a brain tumor the previous year; his mother had died of stomach cancer when he was only six. He had learned that the bonds tethering us to this world were so fragile, and his mistrust of those bonds energized his devil-may-care attitude. Before he got sick, Merton had spent a school holiday hiking all by himself through Germany's Rhine Valley, reading what he called "immoral novels" before developing an infection under a toenail that led to his illness. I wouldn't blame Merton if he thought death was stalking him and his family. Only a few years later, his younger brother John Paul, in his early twenties, would die fighting in World War II. Yet Merton never seemed to reach a point of saying, "This is all too much."

Sometimes, on the subject of death, Merton sounded like he was still that teenager, thumbing his nose at it. He was nearly forty-eight when he wrote, "I am still too young mentally to be in the least patient of any sign of age. My impatience is felt as an upheaval of resentment, disgust, depression. And yet I am joyful. I like life, I am happy with it, I have really nothing to complain of. But a little of the chill, a little of the darkness, the sense of void in the midst of myself, and I say to my body: 'OK, all right then, *die* [double underlined], you idiot!' But it is not really trying to die, it just wants to slow down."

Within the same year, Merton was writing about premonitions of his own death in a way that reflected his Christian beliefs as well as the acceptance of death he'd learned from the Zen and Buddhist beliefs he had been studying: "I think sometimes that I may soon die, though I am not yet old (forty-seven). I don't know exactly what kind of conviction this thought carries with it or what I mean by it. Death is always a possibility for everyone. We live in the presence of this possibility. So I have a habitual awareness that I may die, and that, if this is God's will, then I am glad. 'Go ye forth to meet Him.' And in the light of this I realize the futility of my cares and preoccupations."

Merton appreciated the Eastern concept of nonattachment, which, instead of avoiding the existence of death, uses the full acceptance of it as a way to honor the darkness and the light while enjoying and appreciating the fullness of life: "The autumn quality of detachment that comes from the sense that we are coming to the end of our lives. . . . But this sense of being suspended over nothingness and yet in life, of being a fragile thing, a flame that may blow out, and yet burns brightly, add an inexpressible sweetness to the gift of life, for one sees it entirely and purely as a gift. And one which one must treasure in great fidelity, with a truly pure heart."

In these words and in my experience, however, I find death becomes a tangled paradox, one I'm trying to unravel. Even as I want to enjoy the sweetness Merton describes, I do feel the sense of being suspended over the nothingness. How do

I walk in the glow of this life even as I sense my own death gently approaching? How can I not be discouraged when the loved ones walking with me are lost along the way?

The hardest thing about this learning is that so much of it has to be done on the fly. Sometimes it feels like I'm jumping from an airplane and stitching together my parachute on the way down. I know my thinking may be inconsistent, as yours could be, Thomas, on any given day. It depends on what fresh grief has appeared on the journey. It depends on the turbulence in the air and perhaps even my soul. I'm feeling my way through, but at the same time, I need you to model for me: Help me untie the knots. Help me find the grace in this falling.

PREPARING FOR JOURNEYS

In 1968, a change in leadership at Gethsemani meant Merton had a new abbot, one who was willing to let him travel. He was allowed to accept an invitation to speak at a conference in Bangkok, Thailand, and also to visit other Asian locales to meet and learn from noted Buddhist monks. He joyfully went about planning an itinerary that would take him first to conferences in New Mexico, Alaska, and California and then, as he wrote to his friend Mark Van Doren, "And then, man, I fly to Asia. Really, that is the plan. All sorts of places I am supposed to go to if I don't faint from delight at the mere thought." The places included Calcutta, New Delhi, Dharamsala (where he would meet the Dalai Lama), and Bangkok. Merton spent months getting the proper paperwork and vaccines and writing to his friends to raise funds so that he could travel as widely and comfortably as possible.

I find it interesting that Merton packed and cleaned up the hermitage as though he wouldn't return, the same way he did before leaving for his back surgery in 1966. He emptied overstuffed files, cleared the shelves of books he wasn't taking with him, and notably, burned all of M.'s letters. Yes, his abbot had told him the hermitage might be used by other monks after he left. Yet this seemed like more than a tidying up. Just as in 1966, Merton wasn't taking it for granted that he would return.

If we think about life and death as a journey, then preparation—or, as the phrase goes, getting one's affairs in order—is how one would begin. Merton, well aware of the fact that as a man in his fifties, he could drop dead at any time, had been working on preparations for over a year. The loss of college friends prompted his diligence. "I wonder if any of our bunch will live much beyond sixty," he writes in his journal. That September, a friend from his Columbia days, John Slate, died of a heart attack at age fifty-four. A Columbia classmate, the noted painter Ad Reinhardt, had died only two weeks before, and another, Sy Freedgood, would die in January 1968. "I read the news of Slate's death, around noon, and walked up and down in the sun trying to comprehend it," Merton writes. "I know I too must go soon and must get things in order. Making a will is not enough, and getting manuscripts in order is not enough."

Despite setbacks (Slate was actually supposed to help with the will), Merton managed to get the will done and also recruited a team of friends to be trustees to handle his literary estate and posthumous publishing life. He named Bellarmine

College as the repository of his papers, and the school established the Thomas Merton Center in 1969. I wonder if completing these preparations provided some serenity for Merton. A few months later, eight months before his trip to Asia, he became severely ill with the flu, and he seemed to endure it with little anxiety: "An experience like this sickness is purifying and renewing because it reminds you not to be too attached to the narrow view of what you think life is—the immediate task, the business of getting done what you think is important, of enjoying what you want right now, etc. Sickness pulls the rug from under all of it. Haven't been able to do anything, think anything. Yet in the evening—the bare trees against the metallic blue of the evening were incredibly beautiful: as suspended in a kind of Buddhist emptiness."

I wonder what Thomas would say if he could see how much people put off this kind of preparation. Martin Luther King Jr., Prince, Kurt Cobain, Amy Winehouse, Stieg Larsson: all died without wills. I remember being stunned by how many of the investment executives who died in the World Trade Center terrorist attack of 9/11 did not have life insurance and had left their families in financial binds. My husband and I, since marrying, have always had life insurance, thanks to my older brother who sells it, but we didn't have a will until after my son was born. Not facing this work, I suppose, is another way of holding death at arm's length until life provides an unavoidable kick in the rear. In the early days of the COVID-19 pandemic, lawyers and online legal sites experienced a rush of people wanting to draw up their wills. I'm sure the numbers will eventually drop off again as we move as hastily as possible back to that safe space where we don't have to think about death.

THE LANDSCAPE OF GRIEF

I don't think I fear death. Some aspect of its mystery went away for me after my father died. I was twenty-four, and he was seventy-one. It seemed like if he could manage it, so could I. Something of that sense still remains in me, but I feel it shifting, as though I must come to a new kind of knowing. I'm realizing it's one thing to find a way of thinking about your own death, but it's something else entirely to absorb the loss of contemporaries. It's the deaths that happen around you that rock your core. My friends are dying and, it seems to me, too soon. There are still children to raise, love to discover, work to be done, art to create, books to be written. So much left behind. This is where faith is supposed to help, to be a comfort, but these days I have to work hard to keep from feeling like death is a betrayal. I'm not a swearing person, but when a friend suffers an untimely demise, I want to say to God, "WTF?! What's this all about then? Why fight to live if this is the result?" I'm just a few steps from being Thomas as a teenager. I want to say, "Fine. I don't care." I never really come to that. But I've come close.

Over the years, I have lost my father and a sister, and I've walked with my son through loss after the horrendous mass shootings at his school, Sandy Hook Elementary. Two years ago, my close friends Katy, an award-winning audiobook narrator, and Rob, a talented executive coach and photographer who shot my author photos, both died of cancer. The death of the Christian writer Rachel Held Evans at age thirty-seven, with whom I'd been a speaker at conferences, floored me.

But with Katy's death, something broke, ended, and began all at once. Losing her brought me to my knees. I had such a hope of life for her. She'd been married for less than seven years. She had wanted to have children. She had wanted to grow old. Where do these dreams that never materialize go? I think I'm looking for the place. I feel driven to map out this landscape of grief, that I must come to know it intimately. I know there's no way out of it. In one way or another, I will always be walking here.

My mother died only a few months before the rise of the COVID-19 pandemic. She'd had dementia for years, and in the months leading up to her death, she'd battled a couple of infections. During the same period, many friends lost parents, aunts, uncles, siblings within just a few weeks. Two of my high school classmates had funerals for parents the same weekend as my mom's. I think something is forgotten now in the wake of the coronavirus deaths. But well before the first US diagnosis of this disease that struck the elderly at alarming rates, it felt to me as if the ancestors were taking flight. They were leaving this mess to us. They were done, had seen enough.

After I received the call that my mother had died, the prayers in my mind were to her. I was saying, "You did it!" She had told me a few years ago that she felt her body winding down but didn't know how to let go. Now she had finally done it. I wasn't sad. It was time. Earlier that week, one of my sisters had texted to us siblings photos of our mother. In one of them, she was supposedly awake, but Mom wasn't there. Not really. Her eyes were so empty. I was glad her journey was done, that she didn't have to be in a nursing home anymore, living as a shell of what she once was. I'm content she found a way to move on to the next thing, the next place, and she who had always demonstrated the most steadfast faith now is enjoying the glory of God's face. This is what it means to die in the Lord. Isn't that why, upon hearing of a fellow monk's death, Thomas's practice—that of the whole abbey, really—was to cry out "Alleluia!"?

WINTER AT GETHSEMANI

In December, the month after my mother died, I arrived at the Abbey of Gethsemani in the rain. It was late Friday afternoon, and I had driven myself in a rental car from the Louisville airport. I was too tired to have any expectations. To be honest, I had almost canceled the trip. This would be my third in less than a month, including the travel because of my mother's death. I thought hard about staying home in Connecticut, where there was snow on the ground, and sleeping a good chunk of the weekend. December has become a tough month to navigate, its days marked by decline and loss: The anniversary of the Sandy Hook shootings. My father's final decline, which had begun in December. The same for Katy and Rob. Now my mother was newly gone.

The month of December had been pivotal for Merton as well. He had entered the abbey on December 10, 1941. In December 1959, he received that discouraging no from Rome, denying his request to move to a Mexican monastery. He died on December 10, 1968.

I finally decided that, as emotionally and physically tired as I was, a weekend retreat was what I needed, a silent break where I wouldn't have to talk to anyone or do anything. I had my little rectangular piece of paper with the prayer and meal schedule for the weekend, and I figured that was all I needed. I would pray the Office, eat, and if the weather improved, go for a hike or two. The abbey website had said the hermitage wasn't open to the public, so I didn't even bother to ask to see the place where Merton had lived the last years of his life.

That evening, I ate the best toasted cheese sandwich (on homemade bread) I'd ever had in my life. I listened to the opening retreat talk delivered by a monk, and then I went to my room and fell asleep, waking to my alarm for the 3:15 a.m. Vigils prayer service. I prayed wearing my slippers and sweatpants. The church is designed to feel expansive, with clean, straight lines. The wood of the pews where the monks sat was pale and buttery. The walls of the sanctuary, painted white, had a texture that made them look like a soft cotton blanket.

I spent Saturday as planned, staying in my room except for meals and prayer. I wasn't sure what else I could do, because I felt very aware of the abbey's rules and boundaries. I didn't want to break the former or step over the latter. The huge monastery walls loomed large. My windows looked out over the enclosed garden, and I could see a monk sitting on a bench underneath a tree. I felt like I was spying.

A LANGUAGE OF SILENCE

I think about what my friend Breena said at a colleague's funeral we had attended together. "We all die," she said. "Why do we act so shocked and surprised when it happens?" The fact that Breena, who had lost her beautiful son several years earlier when he was just a teenager, could say this struck me deeply. Her wise words are imprinted in my being, and I wonder if it's all that needs to be said about death. Sometimes, in thinking about death, I feel like I've spilled out all the words that could possibly express even an inkling of the emotion I'm trying to relate. Then that's it. Nothing left in the tank. That's all I can give. But I know the void is deeper, and only silence now can represent it. I think we all feel and fear the silence. Merton writes, "Never has man's helplessness in the face of death been more potable than in this age when he can do everything except escape death.... We are always holding death at arms length, unconsciously trying to think ourselves out of its presence, and this generates an intolerable tension that makes us all the more quickly its victims. It is he who does not fear death who is more ready to escape it and when the time comes, he faces it well."

Merton never got to choose how to face imminent death. The silence fell upon him suddenly, and he died quickly. He had given his talk in the morning at the conference in Bangkok and then went to his room to rest before the evening sessions. When he didn't return, his fellow monks opened his room and found him dead on the floor. Apparently he had stepped out of the shower and been electrocuted after touching a faulty fan.

"Now my whole being breathes the wind that blows through the belfry and my hand is on the door through which I see the heavens," Merton wrote sixteen years earlier. "The door swings out upon a vast sea of darkness and of prayer. Will it come like this, the moment of my death? Will You open a door upon the great forest and set my feet upon a ladder under the moon and take me out among the stars?"

Merton's lifelong friend Mark Van Doren wrote an obituary that observed, "An immense amount of life went out of the world when Thomas Merton died suddenly in Bangkok. . . . He will be missed as few persons of his time will be. His death was more than a blow; it was heartbreaking. . . . That he did not come back [from Asia] is more terrible than I can say." Merton's body was shipped home in a plane carrying the bodies of soldiers, casualties of Vietnam.

I've seen a photo from your requiem mass, Thomas. Your simple coffin is in the center of Gethsemani's church. Your brothers are enrobed in white and sitting in a circle around you. The white walls of the sanctuary seem to embrace the silence. You were only fifty-three.

LISTENING BEYOND THE VEIL

Then slowly, in unexpected ways, the boundaries of my Gethsemani experience seemed to dissolve.

One day near the end of my stay, I was speaking with a monk who happened to be staffing the lobby desk in the retreat house. He asked me where I was from and what I did. When I said I was a writer, he told me about Brother Paul, a poet who had been one of Merton's novices. I realized this was the same man a friend had recommended I meet if I could. I said yes, I would like very much to talk to Brother Paul. The monk took a small sheet of scrap paper from the desk and handed me a pen. "Just leave him a note here," he instructed.

Around nine the next morning, Brother Paul knocked on my door.

We found an empty conference room for our talk. I liked Brother Paul right away. There is something of a spark about him. He seemed to enjoy being in conversation with a new person and a writer. I'm not sure why, but I felt impelled to ask Brother Paul what he missed about Merton. He seemed a little taken aback by the question. I'm not sure if he thought it too personal, or maybe he'd never thought about it at all. Maybe, because of his faith, he didn't really miss the departed in the way others might. But he did give me an answer. He talked about how smart Merton had been. He had enjoyed the man's humor, his quick wit. Yes. It sounded so right. I thanked him for sharing his words with me.

Later that morning, I happened to be in the lobby of the guesthouse when some visitors, not on retreat, came in and asked to see Merton's grave. It turns out the area of his grave was not off limits as I'd thought. A monk at the desk directed them through the glass doors on the opposite side of the room that led out into a garden. I lingered in the lobby, looking at postcards and waiting for the group to leave. When I saw them heading for the parking lot, I went through the doors myself. High gray clouds. Yellowed grass at my feet. I zipped up my coat and stuffed my hands in my pockets.

The white crosses in the monks' cemetery are small and unremarkable, like they could be blown over with ease, but each one stands strong and straight. I had no trouble finding Merton's. It was draped with rosary beads. A red rose was stuck in the ground behind it, and a plastic pink rose had been stuck through the rosary beads, but it was tipped upside down. The flat brown rectangle on the cross reads,

FR. LOUIS MERTON
DIED DEC. 10, 1968

Thomas, when I saw your grave, I cried. I thought of how it had been another December, eight years ago, when I first heard your words and how my journey had brought me through so much to be there at your grave. I looked out over the garden walks, and this aching void welled up within me. I wanted to be on those paths with you, and I mourned you as a friend.

I chastised myself for being so unreasonable. Even if you hadn't died in 1968, it's highly unlikely you would have been alive now. You would have been 105 in January! And yet some aspect of me missed and continues to miss you deeply, aching for a rapport that would challenge us both. Something is breaking my heart again and again. Or perhaps it's just breaking open? You probably would laugh at this, even tease me if you could. But I know you would understand.

WHAT STAYS WITH US

In July 1967, one of Merton's closest friends, Victor Hammer, was lying in a hospital bed, critically ill and dying. The eighty-five-year-old artist, who lived in nearby Lexington, would eventually die that October. Merton writes, "Have thought very much about him all the time. Death is shocking in anyone, but most shocking in the case of someone of real genius and quality and someone you know and love well. The blunt fact is that it is just not conceivable that Victor Hammer should cease to exist."

I think the shock of losing friends is more like a sense of reckoning. We confront their ceasing to exist, knowing it will soon be the same for us. But I don't agree that they are completely gone. In my car, I listen over and over to my friend Katy's reading of the audiobook version of *Pride and Prejudice*. When I speak of her to strangers, I make sure to tell them she was an award-winning audiobook narrator and is in the narrator's hall of fame. I want them to know that something of her humanity is still here and that it's absolutely beautiful.

Watching the film *Bohemian Rhapsody*, I sat in the theater enjoying the depiction of the life of Queen's Freddie Mercury. But I also had this strange undercurrent of feeling that kept saying something like, "That's not him, that's not him, that's not him." I've never felt that before watching a biopic. I didn't realize how strong the feeling was until a video of the real Freddie Mercury singing "Don't Stop Me Now" appeared as the end credits rolled and my heart seemed to take a big sigh of relief. "Ah," it seemed to be saying. "There he is." I think I'd forgotten how much I'd loved him. When Freddie Mercury died in 1991 I felt a quiet, gentle mourning like you might feel at the rise of a brilliant golden moon, one you want to stay close to the earth and glowing forever only to watch it slide away in tiny increments until it is pale and high and far from you. His bandmate Brian May, years later at the unveiling of a statue of Freddie, remarked on how strange it was that the statue, this physical representation, was there and his friend was not. But does Freddie still exist because so many people still love him?

There's something else—something that makes us acknowledge that the veil between "there" and "not there" is thin. Sometimes I sense it—a sheer and soft glittering fabric wrapped around all of us. It holds us close. My son once said of his friend Ben, a six-year-old who died in the Sandy Hook shootings, that we have more of Ben now than ever before. Now Ben is everywhere. Tain has even dreamed of talking to him.

When Tain first told me this, we talked about the different ways we've sensed around us the people we've lost. Then I said, "But you know what? I don't feel that way about Aunt Theo." My sister Theodora, less than a year younger than me, had died the month before her forty-fourth birthday. She was funny, mischievous. If she was present anywhere after her death, I thought, she'd be off bugging someone else, because she had bigger fish to fry. Tain and I had that conversation on a Wednesday. The following Sunday morning, I received a text from my nephew Michael, the adult son of my older brother. Michael had been scanning his bookshelves, looking for something to read, and happened to pull out a book, *The Traveler's Gift*, I had given to Theo several weeks before her death. I'd written an inscription to her in the book, and its pages were covered with her handwritten notes, which showed she had read it. Michael felt impelled to take pictures of these pages. He texted the images to me and said, "Aunt Theo wants you to know she loves you."

How can I read those words and not know there's something more? Even if I'll never know exactly what it is, there is something more. And I will share this: I think I had a similar experience with Thomas Merton—a tap on the shoulder, if you will—at Gethsemani.

MERTON EVERYWHERE

My conversation with Brother Paul led to something so unexpected that I could hardly fathom it: an invitation to the hermitage. He told me a small group of Merton enthusiasts that met regularly would be at the hermitage later that day to celebrate the anniversary of Merton's arrival at Gethsemani. They would enjoy a simple potluck supper together and read aloud from Merton's work. I heartily accepted. He'd let someone know to give me a ride, since I wouldn't know how to get there.

On Sunday evening after the Vespers prayer service, I waited for a monk who could show me to the hermitage. It was dark when we arrived, but the windows of the hermitage were filled with light. I sat for a moment before getting out of the car. I felt a quiet, lovely thrumming in my being, and I just wanted to acknowledge it.

This whole day, it had seemed like something—was it Merton?—was conspiring in my favor to bring me to his grave, his woods, and now his home. Maybe he had been there in my room the day before, watching me reading and going dutifully to the prayers and trying to chant the Psalms. I bet he was shaking his head and laughing at me: *This isn't what you came for. Come on, let's go.* It felt as though he wanted me to see not just the church but everything of what the abbey had been to him.

The hermitage's cinder block walls reminded me of the elementary school I had attended as a girl in Ohio. But there were touches of beauty: bricks with leaf-shaped patterns.

The stone of the fireplace, some of it blackened with smoke. Candles on the mantel.

The group was just beginning to read when I arrived. It was such fun hearing others read Merton's work out loud and talk about what they loved about him. When it was my turn, I read what made the most sense to me to read: the excerpt that had brought me to him. I read the "How the valley awakes" excerpt from *Conjectures of a Guilty Bystander*, the excerpt from the pages torn from that library book eight years earlier.

When we were done and cleaning up so that Brother Paul could get back for Benediction and Compline, I took a last, slow glance around. Oh, Thomas. Your fireplace. Your tiny kitchen. The small cell of a space that served as your bedroom.

"You look like you're looking for someone," a woman from the group said.

I only smiled. Didn't she realize you were still there?

PICTURING TOMORROW

In *Conjectures of a Guilty Bystander*, in the section before the one where Merton talks about his notion that he may soon die, he describes an ethereal dream: "I was lost in a great city and was walking 'toward the center' without quite knowing where I was going. Suddenly I came to a dead end, but on a height, looking at a great bay, an arm of the harbor."

While in Asia, Merton indulged his love of photography, shooting images that would eventually illustrate his *Asian Journal* using a camera loaned to him by his friend the writer and photographer John Howard Griffin. Merton would send

Griffin his rolls of film, and Griffin would develop them and provide Merton with contact sheets and notes on what he thought were the best shots. After Merton died, Griffin, upon learning the camera would be returned to him, guessed that it might contain photographs. He wrote a letter to the powers that be, begging them not to open the camera when it went through customs. It turned out he had guessed right. "More carefully than I have ever done anything in my life, I removed that roll of film," writes Griffin.

There were eighteen images on the roll of film, and Griffin describes the first photograph that he chose to enlarge. It showed a harbor lined with boats, the water shimmering with light: "I looked through Merton's eyes on a scene viewed from some high place, downward past the edge of a building and a foreground of shore across a broad body of water from which reflected sunlight glinted back into the viewer's eyes—a universal, all-embracing view of men and boats and water, seen from the perspective of height and distance." Only later did Griffin realize this image of the Bangkok River was an exact depiction of the dream Merton had written about years before.

I find comfort in this story, Thomas—in the fact that you dreamed, years earlier, of the place that would hold your vision right before your death. For as much as we seek our paths and have questions about the journey, there is a sense deep within us, like a primeval compass, that shows we already know where to go. We only have to recognize the place, live our lives trusting it is there, and believe, when the time comes to float toward the harbor, that all shall be well.

Sometimes I dream of a place I've never been, yet it seems so deeply familiar. It looks like a seaside in Britain, because the ocean is vast in front of me, and the buildings behind me, though I can't see them, seem to be made of very old brick and stone. There's something different about the place—it radiates a warm and gentle glow, like the golden hour of light in that precious time right before the sun begins to set. And though I see no one directly, I know I'm not alone. The place feels spacious yet full all at once. And though I'm standing there, it feels like a place I'm going to—a place pulling me homeward. Pulling me into safe harbor.

My whole life feels like a course toward this place. It's a joyful feeling, like I'm a child running on sandy shores. I know I will recognize this harbor when I arrive, when I come to this place where frothy blue water meets luscious golden light.

Acknowledgments

THE WRITING OF THIS BOOK WAS FUNDED IN PART BY an Artist Fellowship Grant from the Connecticut Office of the Arts, which also receives funding from the National Endowment for the Arts, a federal agency. I am grateful for the recognition and support of my work.

A huge thanks to Lynn Domina and Dave Harrity, my copanelists discussing Merton at the Festival of Faith and Writing, and to the woman whose name I don't know who came up to me later at the festival and gave me a light bulb moment when she said something like "You're writing your Merton book, right?" I wasn't then. Thanks to her, I have now.

I'm grateful to Nancy Lynne Westfield of the Wabash Center and Willie James Jennings of Yale Divinity School for vital conversations that helped develop my thinking as I worked on the book's proposal and to Barbara Brown Taylor, who read that proposal and sent encouraging words.

Thanks to the monks and staff of the Abbey of Our Lady of Gethsemani, especially Father Seamus, Father Michael, Father Carlos, Everistus Okinor, and of course, Brother Paul Quenon. I hope to return soon.

My visit to the Thomas Merton Center at Bellarmine University allowed me to see Merton's handwriting in one of his journals. I know that may seem like a small thing, but as someone who still writes a lot by hand myself, this was another level of connection to Merton for me. I'm grateful the center does such a wonderful job of maintaining his legacy. Also, on the center's website, I found a document that was absolutely indispensable to me in writing this book: Patricia A. Burton's *Merton Vade Mecum: A Quick-Reference Bibliographic Handbook* (4th ed., Louisville: Thomas Merton Center, 2016). This document places Merton's publication dates, as well as the dates of significant events in his life, in the specific time frame of each journal entry. Since I was working so closely with Merton's journals and sought to have my book, to some degree, follow the timeline of Merton's life, I referred to the *Vade Mecum* constantly.

My editor, Valerie Weaver-Zercher, has been for me what every writer hopes to have—a thoughtful, supportive, and wise voice who can see a book from the big-picture organization level all the way down to the more specific, minute levels involving detail, sentence structure, and beauty. She is sublime. Thank you, Valerie.

I'm grateful for my agent, Brettne Bloom, and for her willingness to travel the twists and turns of this writing journey with me.

Thanks to Sterling Memorial Library at Yale University, where a good deal of the work on this book was done. And thanks to the students and teachers of Berkeley Divinity, the Episcopal Seminary at Yale Divinity School, for allowing me to share morning prayer, tea, and conversation with them at the Berkeley Center.

To William R. Smith: thank you for your "There's your boy" comment—that meant more than you realized.

To Darryl and Tain: tremendous gratitude for your love and patience when I was spending more time with the book than I was with both of you.

Acknowledgments

I have received such love and support as I worked on this project, and I hope the following will see their love reflected in the book's pages: Brian Allain, Anupama Amaran, Sarah Arthur, Diana Butler Bass, Mathieu Cailler, Kathryn Greene-McCreight, David Hicks, Heather Jackson, Janet Labati, Phoebe Farag Mikhail, Donald Quist, my friends at River Pretty Writers Retreat, Kali VanBaale, Robert Vivian, and Peter Wright.

Finally, I would be remiss if I didn't offer gratitude here for Thomas Merton, the monk who follows me around and gives me advice. When I was walking the trails on the property of the Abbey of Our Lady of Gethsemani, I came upon a statue of the Blessed Virgin Mary. She's made of white stone and created to look straight and tall and heavy, like a pillar. But the statue is perched on the block of marble in such a way that it looks as if it's floating just above the block and over the edge. The plaque with the sculptor's name, Forrest Robisch, says, "She walks with God." Heavenly steps indeed. Are you on such a walk now, Thomas? Are you everywhere, as my son suggests of those who have left us? Are you here in my office, even as your spirit walks the woods of Gethsemani?

The following words are on another plaque at the base of the statue. I offer them to you now, Thomas, in hopes you will remain an element of my everywhere and continue your gentle guidance on my path:

For all that has been . . .
Thanks.
To all that shall be . . .
Yes.

Notes

CHAPTER 1

1 *"Of one thing I am certain"*: All epigraphs from Thomas Merton.

2 *"a thinker who challenged"*: Pope Francis, *Address*.

3 *"The first chirps"*: Merton, *Conjectures*, 127.

4 *"Here is an unspeakable secret"*: Merton, *Conjectures*, 127.

5 *"I learned he was born"*: Knight, "Thomas Merton."

6 *"overwhelmed with a sudden"*: Merton, *Seven Storey Mountain*, 122–23.

8 *"Thomas. What's yours?"*: Merton, April 1940, *Run to the Mountain*, 1:196.

8 *"This morning"*: Merton, November 9, 1958, *Search for Solitude*, 3:228.

9 *"I suppose if Melville Cain"*: Merton, January 24, 1940, *Run to the Mountain*, 1:145.

9 *"There are a lot of things"*: Merton, November 10, 1940, *Run to the Mountain*, 1:252.

9 *"I have a natural tendency"*: Merton, June 5, 1960, *Turning toward the World*, 4:8.

10 *"I have certainly not been"*: Merton, May 26, 1963, *Turning toward the World*, 4:324.

11 *"I have no intention"*: Merton, May 11, 1967, *Learning to Love*, 6:234.

12 *"The ever-changing reality"*: Merton, *New Seeds of Contemplation*, 14.

12 *"This power of non-deceiving"*: Merton, June 13, 1959, *Search for Solitude*, 3:292.

13 *"His life became"*: Kidd, "False Self, True Self," x.

CHAPTER 2

17 *"And so within three days":* Merton, *Seven Storey Mountain*, 422.

19 *"Our trouble is that":* Merton, *Seeds of Destruction*, 25.

20 *"Americans spend $1.2 trillion":* Becker, *Minimalist Home*, 13.

20 *"The great sin":* Merton, April 17, 1965, *Dancing in the Water*, 5:230.

21 *"The overwhelming welter":* Merton, December 13, 1958, *Search for Solitude*, 3:238.

24 *"[He] has (like a million others)":* Merton, August 22, 1961, *Turning toward the World*, 4:154–55.

25 *"Meditation on the automobile":* Merton, *Conjectures*, 70.

26 *"Stanch in me the rank wound":* Merton, *New Seeds of Contemplation*, 44–45.

28 *"I had on only my Trappist overalls":* Merton, May 7, 1966, *Learning to Love*, 6:52.

28 *"Knowing when you do not need":* Merton, May 19, 1961, *Turning toward the World*, 4:119.

30 *"We pride ourselves":* Merton, January 19, 1959, *Search for Solitude*, 3:248.

CHAPTER 3

35 *"My chief concern":* Merton, *Seven Storey Mountain*, 259.

36 *"I miss my novel":* Merton, January 26, 1940, *Run to the Mountain*, 1:148.

36 *"This was what I really":* Merton, *Seven Storey Mountain*, 259.

36 *"How could I love God":* Merton, *Seven Storey Mountain*, 259.

37 *"Of course, as far as":* Merton, *Seven Storey Mountain*, 253.

38 *"hid his face":* Merton, *Seven Storey Mountain*, 414.

38 *"there was this shadow":* Merton, *Seven Storey Mountain*, 448.

39 *"He rides my shoulders":* Merton, *Seven Storey Mountain*, 448.

39 *"[He] decided that":* Merton, *Sign of Jonas*, 90.

40 *"writing carefully and well":* Merton, April 16, 1947, *Entering the Silence*, 2:63.

40 *"As usual I have to check":* Merton, April 25, 1948, *Entering the Silence*, 2:199.

40 **"I caught myself thinking":** Merton, July 11, 1948, *Entering the Silence*, 2:218.

40 **"We do not know":** Merton, January 26, 1948, *Entering the Silence*, 2:161.

41 **"Someone accused me":** Merton, January 19, 1961, *Turning toward the World*, 4:86–87.

41 **"It brought me again":** Merton, October 27, 1961, *Turning toward the World*, 4:174.

42 **"The root of the trouble":** Merton, July 20, 1963, *Turning toward the World*, 4:341.

43 **"All day I have been":** Merton, March 10, 1965, *Dancing in the Water*, 5:216.

44 **"I will never fulfill":** Merton, October 2, 1958, *Search for Solitude*, 3:220–21.

45 **"Do anything that pleases you":** Taylor, *Altar in the World*, 110.

45 **"It was not what I did":** Taylor, *Altar in the World*, 110.

47 **"I love the people":** Merton, *Sign of Jonas*, 89–90.

48 **"In religious terms":** Merton, "First and Last Thoughts," 16–17.

CHAPTER 4

50 **"The waking of crows":** Merton, *Conjectures*, 128.

51 **"The expansiveness and depth":** Merton, *Entering the Silence*, 2:328.

51 **"Once beyond":** Hinkle and Weis, *Thomas Merton's Gethsemani*, 44.

52 **"As soon as I get away":** Merton, June 27, 1949, *Entering the Silence*, 2:328.

53 **"And I thought":** Merton, June 27, 1949, *Entering the Silence*, 2:329.

54 **"How absolutely central":** Merton, *Conjectures*, 296.

55 **"The Spirit of God":** Merton, *Entering the Silence*, 2:329.

56 **"the marvelous quiet!":** Merton, *Entering the Silence*, 2:329.

56 **"Again, sense of the importance":** Merton, May 31, 1961, *Turning toward the World*, 4:123.

59 **"Brilliant afternoon":** Merton, May 2, 1961, *Turning toward the World*, 4:114.

59 **"Well, another torrent":** Merton, June 15, 1961, *Turning toward the World*, 4:127 (Merton's capitalization).

59 **"Weather hot as midsummer":** Merton, May 19, 1962, *Turning toward the World*, 4:219.

59 **"A brilliant Saturday":** Merton, July 21, 1962, *Turning toward the World*, 4:232.

59 **"Cold wind":** Merton, December 6, 1962, *Turning toward the World*, 4:271.

59 **"Very cold morning":** Merton, January 21, 1963, *Turning toward the World*, 4:291.

59 **"Our mentioning":** Merton, February 27, 1963, *Turning toward the World*, 4:299–300.

61 **"When I thought the gardenias":** Merton, August 11, 1961, *Turning toward the World*, 4:150.

61 **"Pure dark sky":** Merton, January 21, 1963, *Turning toward the World*, 4:291.

61 **"Hawk. First shadow":** Merton, July 23, 1962, *Turning toward the World*, 4:233.

62 **"With the new":** Merton, February 17, 1966, *Learning to Love*, 6:19.

64 **"Gethsemani looked beautiful":** Merton, *Entering the Silence*, 2:329.

64 **"If we instinctively seek":** Merton, *Mystics and Zen Masters*, 111.

CHAPTER 5

66 **"I was suddenly overwhelmed":** Merton, *Conjectures*, 153–54.

66 **"from cloister toward world":** Merton, *Turning toward the World*, 4:xix.

66 **"one of the most famous":** Erickson, "Thomas Merton's Mystical Vision."

67 **"Was in Louisville Thursday":** Merton, August 15, 1959, *Search for Solitude*, 3:316.

68 **"Everything in me cries out":** Merton, April 6, 1949, *Entering the Silence*, 2:301.

69 **"I think it is better":** Merton, July 25, 1959, *Search for Solitude*, 3:310.

69 **"Yesterday I was bitter":** Merton, May 18, 1959, *Search for Solitude*, 3:282.

70 **"I really want to do":** Merton, May 10, 1959, *Search for Solitude*, 3:279.

Notes

70 **"Is the freedom precious":** Merton, June 11, 1959, *Search for Solitude*, 3:291.

71 **"Perhaps what is upsetting":** Merton, June 18, 1959, *Search for Solitude*, 3:296.

72 **"There is the level of faith":** Merton, April 29, 1961, *Turning toward the World*, 4:113.

73 **"I think the chief reason":** Merton, February 5, 1950, *Entering the Silence*, 2:406.

73 **"Always the old trouble":** Merton, September 30, 1963, *Dancing in the Water*, 5:20.

75 **"I honestly begin to wonder":** Merton, December 27, 1958, *Search for Solitude*, 3:240.

76 **"I will follow my conscience":** Merton, January 25, 1959, *Search for Solitude*, 3:251.

76 **"In the afternoon-evening":** Merton, January 24, 1966, *Learning to Love*, 6:12.

CHAPTER 6

79 **"had banded themselves together":** Merton, *Seven Storey Mountain*, 383.

80 **"I needed this support":** Merton, *Seven Storey Mountain*, 383.

80 **"In the early Celtic church":** O'Donohue, *Anam Cara*, xviii.

81 **"With other writers":** Merton to Boris Pasternak, October 23, 1958, *Courage for Truth*, 89.

81 **"wonderfully filled with":** Merton, *Courage for Truth*, 89.

81 **"confirmed my intuition":** Merton, October 12, 1958, *Search for Solitude*, 3:223–24.

82 **"This simple and human dialogue":** Merton, October 18, 1958, *Search for Solitude*, 3:225.

83 **"Human presence is":** O'Donohue, *Anam Cara*, xvi–xvii.

84 **"earthy man, dressed":** Henri Nouwen's foreword to James Finley's *Merton's Palace of Nowhere*.

85 **"If you stay away":** Rumi in Barks, *Rumi*, 63.

86 **"Particular Friendships":** Mott, *Seven Mountains*, 318.

86 **"[He's] one of the few":** Merton, *Conjectures*, 155.

86 **"Fr. John of the Cross said":** Merton, March 22, 1961, *Turning toward the World*, 4:101.

86 **"I know the integrity":** Merton, *Conjectures*, 155–56.

86 **"What they are continuing":** Merton, March 1, 1959, *Search for Solitude*, 3:265.

89 **"I might not be":** Taylor, *Altar in the World*, xv.

90 **"I will not be so foolish":** Merton to Daisetz T. Suzuki, March 12, 1959, *Hidden Ground of Love*, 561.

91 **"If I should demand":** Merton, April 11, 1959, *Search for Solitude*, 3:273.

92 **"The most important thing is Love":** Mott, *Seven Mountains*, 399.

92 **"One is paid":** Merton, *Conjectures*, 318.

CHAPTER 7

99 **"We're all monks now":** Hillis, "We're All Monks Now."

101 **"The contemplative life":** Merton, *Seeds of Destruction*, xiii.

102 **"The duty of the Christian":** Merton, *Passion for Peace*, 25.

102 **"What had happened to him":** Merton, *Passion for Peace*, 10.

103 **"But the El Grecos":** Merton, *Run to the Mountain*, 1:52.

103 **"These expressions of hatred":** Merton, *Run to the Mountain*, 1:89.

104 **"Ever since my baptism":** Merton, *Run to the Mountain*, 1:121.

106 **"Merton's public image":** Mott, *Seven Mountains*, 371.

106 **"Let us never forget":** *Congressional Record*, April 18, 1962.

107 **"The decision seems to be":** Merton, April 27, 1962, *Turning toward the World*, 4:216.

108 **"If I participate":** Thomas, *How to Preach*, xxi.

108 **"challenges unjust moral orders":** Thomas, *Surviving*, xviii.

109 **"We tend to think":** Merton, September 10, 1960, *Turning toward the World*, 4:44.

110 **"But with things as crazy":** Merton, November 11, 1965, *Dancing in the Water*, 5:314–15.

110 **"The minimal efforts":** Horan, "Merton (Still) Matters."

111 **"It seems to me":** Merton, *Conjectures*, 42–43.

111 **"The conviction that":** Merton, June 22, 1958, *Search for Solitude*, 3:207.

CHAPTER 8

116 *"private prayer":* Merton, *Entering the Silence*, 2:489.

116 *"And that was before publication":* Mott, *Seven Mountains*, 230.

117 *"The answer, his superiors":* Mott, *Seven Mountains*, 230.

118 *"Everything about this hermitage":* Merton, February 24, 1965, *Dancing in the Water*, 5:209.

118 *"It finally helped me":* Merton, October 13, 1964, *Dancing in the Water*, 5:154.

118 *"[I] lit the fire":* Merton, October 13, 1964, *Dancing in the Water*, 5:154.

119 *"At the moment the writing":* Merton, July 20, 1949, *Entering the Silence*, 2:338.

119 *"In this rusted metal chapel":* Hinkle and Weis, *Thomas Merton's Gethsemani*, 73.

120 *"I have my fingers":* Merton, November 16, 1947, *Entering the Silence*, 2:134.

121 *"the cleverest witch":* Rowling, *Harry Potter and the Prisoner of Azkaban*, 346.

121 *"She knows there are interior":* Rowling, *Harry Potter and the Sorcerer's Stone*, 287.

121 *"Do not know where":* Merton, September 3, 1960, *Turning toward the World*, 4:41.

122 *"Intellectuals and artists":* Wiman, *My Bright Abyss*, 63.

123 *"manifest themselves as birds":* Merton, *Conjectures*, 127.

124 *"I realize now how weak":* Merton, May 7, 1959, *Search for Solitude*, 3:278.

125 *"Solitude—when you get":* Merton, *Turning toward the World*, 4:327.

125 *"a treasure chest":* The *Book of Common Prayer*, Episcopal Church, accessed August 7, 2020, https://episcopalchurch.org/book-common-prayer.

125 *"The Lord is good":* Psalm 100:5, *Book of Common Prayer*, 83.

126 *"Arise, shine":* Isaiah 60:1, *Book of Common Prayer*, 87.

127 *"My chapel is plain":* Merton, *Other Side of the Mountain*, April 30, 1968, 7:86.

127 *"Fabulously beautiful":* Merton, *Conjectures*, 298.

128 *"While prayer may often be":* Forest, "Praying with Icons."

Notes

128 **"I never tire of gazing":** Merton to Marco Pallis, December 5, 1965, *Hidden Ground of Love*, 473–74.

130 **"Joy before the ikon":** Merton, March 26, 1962, *Turning toward the World*, 4:21.

133 **"I realize how all around me":** Merton, September 26, 1962, *Turning toward the World*, 4:251.

134 **"Go where your best":** Buechner, *Telling Secrets*, 92.

CHAPTER 9

137 **"Here in this huge":** Merton, *Seven Storey Mountain*, 378.

138 **"Overarching the entire essay":** Hillis, "Letters," 121.

138 **"to become once more":** Cleaver, *Soul on Ice*, 44–45.

138 **"felt alienated":** Hillis, "Letters," 122.

140 **"I'm of mixed race":** Galant, "Man Who Can Explain."

142 **"You have to take":** Hillis, "Letters," 127.

143 **"Where minds are full":** Merton, *Seeds of Destruction*, 7.

143 **"I need to understand":** Merton, October 10, 1960, *Turning toward the World*, 4:57.

146 **"calling Thompson to work":** Hillis, "Letters," 127.

147 **"awaken the conscience":** Merton, *Seeds of Destruction*, 45–46.

147 **"I face the fact":** Merton, April 26, 1967, *Learning to Love*, 6:225.

148 **"He [Baldwin] seems":** Merton, February 23, 1963, *Turning toward the World*, 4:297.

148 **"Our vocation":** Merton, *Raids on the Unspeakable*, 62.

149 **"These Negroes are not":** Merton, *Seeds of Destruction*, 45.

CHAPTER 10

151 **"Yet I know I have to die":** Merton, March 23, 1966, *Learning to Love*, 6:33.

152 **"All I know is":** Merton, April 28, 1966, *Learning to Love*, 6:47.

152 **"Clearly this love":** Merton, May 12, 1966, *Learning to Love*, 6:59.

153 **"I suppose I regret":** Merton, January 30, 1965, *Dancing in the Water*, 5:198.

153 **"Instead of feeling impure":** Merton, May 17, 1966, *Learning to Love*, 6:67.

154 **"I can see that it"**: Merton, May 27, 1966, *Learning to Love*, 6:71.

155 **"M. is . . . in the end"**: Merton, "Midsummer Diary for M.," June 18, 1966, *Learning to Love*, 6:311.

156 **"When you have once"**: Merton, October 16, 1966, *Learning to Love*, 6:150.

156 **"It is one of the most beautiful"**: Merton, October 16, 1966, *Learning to Love*, 6:150.

158 **"love is regarded"**: Merton, *Love and Living*, 29.

158 **"we come to consider"**: Merton, *Love and Living*, 29.

159 **"We cannot help revising"**: Merton, *Love and Living*, 32–33.

159 **"Today, one's security"**: Merton, *Love and Living*, 31.

160 **"Our English expression"**: Merton, *Love and Living*, 25.

160 **"the [person] who is constantly"**: Merton, February 17, 1959, *Search for Solitude*, 3:263.

160 **"He who loves"**: Merton, *Love and Living*, 35–36.

163 **"Was I being faithful"**: Merton, September 4, 1966, *Learning to Love*, 6:121.

CHAPTER 11

166 **"And I lay there"**: Merton, *Seven Storey Mountain*, 107–8.

166 **"I am still too young"**: Merton, October 2, 1962, *Turning toward the World*, 4:253.

167 **"I think sometimes that"**: Merton, *Conjectures*, 186–87.

167 **"The autumn quality"**: Merton, December 15, 1962, *Turning toward the World*, 4:276.

168 **"And then, man, I fly"**: Van Doren, "Thomas Merton's Obituary."

169 **"I wonder if any"**: Merton, September 14, 1967, *Learning to Love*, 6:291.

169 **"I read the news"**: Merton, September 22, 1967, *Learning to Love*, 6:293.

170 **"An experience like this"**: Merton, January 19, 1968, *Other Side of the Mountain*, 7:44.

175 **"Never has man's helplessness"**: Merton, November 25, 1958, *Search for Solitude*, 3:232.

175 **"Now my whole being"**: Merton, July 5, 1952, Fire Watch entry, *Entering the Silence*, 2:486.

176 ***"An immense amount of life":*** Van Doren, "Thomas Merton's Obituary."

178 ***"Have thought very much":*** Merton, July 8, 1967, *Learning to Love*, 6:260–61.

182 ***"I was lost":*** Merton, *Conjectures*, 170–71.

183 ***"More carefully than":*** Griffin and Merton, *Hidden Wholeness*, 144–45.

Bibliography

I list here the writings of Thomas Merton in two sections—the seven journals, according to the order in which he wrote them, and the other published works of Merton's that I consulted. The work of other writers I cite appears in the last section.

JOURNALS OF THOMAS MERTON

Merton, Thomas. *Run to the Mountain: The Story of a Vocation*. Edited by Patrick Hart. Vol. 1 of *The Journals of Thomas Merton*. New York: HarperOne, 1999.

———. *Entering the Silence: Becoming a Monk and a Writer*. Edited by Jonathan Montaldo. Vol. 2 of *The Journals of Thomas Merton*. New York: HarperOne, 1996.

———. *A Search for Solitude: Pursuing the Monk's True Life*. Edited by Lawrence Cunningham. Vol. 3 of *The Journals of Thomas Merton*. New York: HarperOne, 2009.

———. *Turning toward the World: The Pivotal Years*. Edited by Victor A. Kramer. Vol. 4 of *The Journals of Thomas Merton*. New York: HarperOne, 1998.

———. *Dancing in the Water of Life: Seeking Peace in the Hermitage*. Edited by Robert E. Daggy. Vol. 5 of *The Journals of Thomas Merton*. New York: HarperOne, 1998.

———. *Learning to Love: Exploring Solitude and Freedom*. Edited by Christine M. Bochen. Vol. 6 of *The Journals of Thomas Merton*. New York: HarperOne, 2010.

———. *The Other Side of the Mountain: The End of the Journey*. Edited by Patrick Hart. Vol. 7 of *The Journals of Thomas Merton*. New York: HarperOne, 1998.

OTHER WORKS BY THOMAS MERTON

Merton, Thomas. *Conjectures of a Guilty Bystander*. New York: Image Books, 2014.

———. *The Courage for Truth: The Letters of Thomas Merton to Writers*. Edited by Christine M. Bochen. New York: Harvest/HJB, 1994.

———. "First and Last Thoughts: An Author's Preface." In *A Thomas Merton Reader*, edited by Thomas P. McDonnell, 13–18. New York: Image Books Doubleday, 1974.

———. *The Hidden Ground of Love: The Letters of Thomas Merton on Religious Experience and Social Concerns*. Edited by William H. Shannon. New York: Harcourt Brace Jovanovich, 1993.

———. *Love and Living*. Edited by Patrick Hart and Naomi Burton Stone. New York: Harcourt, 1985.

———. *Mystics and Zen Masters*. New York: Farrar, Straus and Giroux, 1999.

———. *New Seeds of Contemplation*. New York: New Directions, 2007.

———. *Passion for Peace: Reflections on War and Nonviolence*. New York: Crossroad, 2006.

———. *Raids on the Unspeakable*. New York: New Directions, 1966.

———. *Seeds of Destruction*. New York: Farrar, Straus and Giroux, 1964.

———. *The Seven Storey Mountain*. New York: Harcourt Brace, 1998.

———. *The Sign of Jonas*. New York: Harcourt, 1981.

OTHER WORKS CITED

Abernathy, Jeff. *To Hell and Back*. Athens: University of Georgia Press, 2017.

Barks, Coleman. *Rumi: The Big Red Book: The Great Masterpiece Celebrating Mystical Love and Friendship*. New York: HarperOne, 2011.

Becker, Joshua, and Eric Stanford. *The Minimalist Home: A Room-by-Room Guide to a Decluttered, Refocused Life*. Colorado Springs: WaterBrook, 2018.

The Book of Common Prayer. London: Ebury, 1992.

Buechner, Frederick. *Telling Secrets*. San Francisco: HarperSanFrancisco, 2004.

Burton, Patricia A., and Patrick F. O'Connell. *Merton Vade Mecum: A Quick-Reference Bibliographic Handbook; Comprising: A Thomas*

Merton Timeline, with Journal Entries in Full, Published Letters,
Publications, Life, Historical Events; Publications List, with Titles of
Merton's Books, Essays, Poetry; Complete with Notes, Appendices.
4th ed. Louisville: Thomas Merton Center, 2016.

Cleaver, Eldridge. *Soul on Ice*. New York: Dell, 1968.

Erickson, Lori. "Thomas Merton's Mystical Vision in Louisville." Spiritual
Travels. Accessed March 14, 2020. https://tinyurl.com/y3qcyxo6.

Forest, Jim. "Praying with Icons: Spiritual Practice." Spirituality and
Practice. Accessed May 5, 2020. https://tinyurl.com/yxfmq37v.

Galant, Richard. "The Man Who Can Explain Everything" CNN.com,
September 1, 2011. https://tinyurl.com/yxdprh6g.

Griffin, John Howard, and Thomas Merton. *A Hidden Wholeness: The*
Visual World of Thomas Merton. Boston: Houghton Mifflin, 1970.

Hillis, Gregory K. "Letters to a Black Catholic Priest: Thomas Merton,
Fr. August Thompson and the Civil Rights Movement." *Merton*
Annual 32 (2019): 114–36.

———. "We're All Monks Now." *America*, April 22, 2020.
https://tinyurl.com/y8yf5hd2.

Hinkle, Harry L., and Monica Weis. *Thomas Merton's Gethsemani: Land-*
scapes of Paradise. Lexington: University Press of Kentucky, 2005.

Horan, Daniel P. "Merton (Still) Matters: How the Trappist Monk and
Author Speaks to Millennials." *America Magazine*, January 19, 2015,
20–23. https://tinyurl.com/yxufmh8c.

Jones, Timothy K. *The Spiritual Formation Bible: Growing in Intimacy with*
God through Scripture: New Revised Standard Version (NRSV). Grand
Rapids, MI: Zondervan, 1999.

Kidd, Sue Monk. "False Self, True Self: Finding the Real Me." In New
Seeds of Contemplation, by Thomas Merton, vii–xiv. New York: New
Directions, 2007.

Knight, Jim. "The Thomas Merton We Knew." Accessed August 7, 2020.
http://www.therealmerton.com/tommie.html.

Mott, Michael. *The Seven Mountains of Thomas Merton*. New York:
Harcourt Brace, 1993.

Nouwen, Henri J. M. Foreword to *Merton's Palace of Nowhere*, by James
Finley, vii–ix. Notre Dame: Ave Maria, 2018.

O'Donohue, John. *Anam Cara: A Book of Celtic Wisdom*. New York:
HarperCollins, 1998.

Bibliography

Pope Francis. *Address of the Holy Father to the Joint Session of the United States Congress.* September 2015. https://tinyurl.com/pmc3hvr.

Rowling, J. K. *Harry Potter and the Prisoner of Azkaban.* New York: Scholastic, 2001.

———. *Harry Potter and the Sorcerer's Stone.* New York: Scholastic, 1999.

Taylor, Barbara Brown. *An Altar in the World: A Geography of Faith.* New York: HarperOne, 2010.

Thomas, Frank A. *How to Preach a Dangerous Sermon.* Nashville: Abingdon, 2018.

———. *Surviving a Dangerous Sermon.* Nashville: Abingdon, 2020.

Van Doren, Mark. "Thomas Merton's Obituary from 1969." *America Magazine,* July 22, 2019. https://tinyurl.com/y5zy8y9u.

Wiman, Christian. *My Bright Abyss: Meditation of a Modern Believer.* New York: Farrar, Straus & Giroux, 2014.